THE STORY OF THE RESTORATION

Bill J. Humble, PhD

Charleston, AR
COBB PUBLISHING
2021

The Story of the Restoration is copyright ©2021 by Cobb Publishing, all rights reserved. No portion of this book may be reproduced (whether in digital, audio, video, print, or any other medium) in any way or shared online without the permission of the publisher.

Published in the United States of America by
Cobb Publishing
704 E. Main St.
Charleston, AR 72933
CobbPublishing@gmail.com
www.CobbPublishing.com
479.747.8372

ISBN: 978-1-947622-75-3

Contents

Chapter 1: Backgrounds and Beginnings 7
   Religion in Colonial America................................. 7
   Two Great Awakenings 11
   The O'Kelly Movement 13
   The New England Christians................................. 15
   Questions for review and discussion 16

Chapter 2: The Stone Movement 18
   Early Life and Ministry.................................... 18
   The Cane Ridge Meeting 20
   The Springfield Presbytery................................. 22
   Problems and Programs 24
   Questions for review and discussion 27

Chapter 3: The Campbell Movement 29
   Thomas Campbell.. 29
   Christian Association of Washington 32
   Alexander Campbell 33
   The Brush Run Church 36
   Questions for Review and Discussion 37

Chapter 4: The Restoration Principle 39
   Unity through restoration 39
   The Restoration Principle in Practice 43
   Problems in application.................................... 46
   Summary 48
   Questions for review and discussion 48

Chapter 5: Reformers among the Baptists 50
   The question of immersion.................................. 50
   Non-Baptist leaven 52

    Walter Scott 54
    The Separation 57
    Questions for review and discussion 59

Chapter 6: The Movements Converge 61

    Similarities 62
    And differences 62
    Unity achieved 64
    A decade of growth 67
    Questions for review and discussion 70

Chapter 7: The Missionary Society Controversy 72

    The cooperation meeting 72
    "The burnt child dreads the fire" 73
    Campbell's call for organization 74
    American Christian Missionary Society 76
    A decade of opposition 79
    Questions for review and discussion 82

Chapter 8: The Civil War Ordeal 84

    Christian pacifism 85
    On record for the Union 88
    A second loyalty resolution 89
    Sectional bitterness 91
    Questions for review and discussion 93

Chapter 9: The Influence of Editors 95

Benjamin Franklin and the *American Christian Review* 95
    Isaac Errett and the *Christian Standard* 97
    David Lipscomb and the *Gospel Advocate* 100
    J. W. McGarvey and Moses Lard 102
    A pivotal year 104
    Questions for review and discussion 104

Chapter 10: The Decade of Decision 106

    The Louisville Plan 106

    The instrumental music controversy 108
    Central Christian Church 112
    Foreign Christian Missionary Society 114
    Questions for review and discussion 115

Chapter 11: The Lines of Division 117

    The progessives win the North 117
    The conservative South 119
    The 1906 census 120
    Why the division? 123
    Liberalism in the Christian Church 124
    Questions for review and discussion 127

Chapter 12: Twentieth Century Growth 128

    Journals 130
    Christian Colleges 131
    Controversial Issues 133
    World Missions 135
    Questions for review and discussion 137

Chapter 13: The Continuing Restoration 140

    Disciples of Christ 140
    "Independent" Christian Churches 142
    Churches of Christ 143
    A Continuing Challenge 146
    Questions for review and discussion 150

Chapter 1
Backgrounds and Beginnings

The Restoration Movement began in America about 1800, nearly 200 years after the first English settlements in the New World. During the two centuries of colonial history many European denominations had been transplanted in America, and it was amidst these older churches, rather than in virgin religious ground, that the Restoration Movement began. The Restoration Movement's role in the drama of America could not be played apart from the backdrop of earlier American church history, and thus it seems essential to sketch this background before introducing the Restoration Movement.

Religion in Colonial America

The European visitor to America in the 1700's would have found one thing most impressive about America's religion – its great diversity as compared with the countries of Europe. This was especially true in the middle colonies like New York and Pennsylvania, where many diverse European nationalities were already becoming a "melting pot." Yet even in Puritan New England and the Anglican South, the state-supported churches had been unable to keep dissenters from settling in their domains.

The Anglican Church (Church of England) is the best example of an "established church" in Europe which enjoyed the same favored status in America. An "established church" is a state-church, i.e., one which is favored by the government and supported by taxation. Virginia was the first English colony in America, and the settlers at Jamestown (1607) were Anglicans, so it is not surprising that Anglicanism became the state-church in Virginia. As other Southern colonies were established, the Anglican Church gained the same privileged status that it occupied in Virginia. The religious history of Maryland is somewhat different from the other Southern colonies, for it was founded by a Catholic, Lord Baltimore. However, Lord Baltimore was forced for political and economic reasons to grant religious toleration to other churches; and in 1649 under a Protestant governor, William Stone, the Maryland legislature adopted a famous Toleration Act. Barton W. Stone, a leader in the Restoration Movement, was a direct descendant of Governor Stone. Late in the 1600's the Protestants gained control of Maryland, denied freedom to the Catholics, and made Anglicanism the established church. At the end of the colonial period the Anglican Church was a state-church in all the Southern colonies, but lost its favored status during the Revolution. In 1784 the Anglican churches in America became the Episcopal Church.

In the New England colonies of Massachusetts, Connecticut and New Hampshire the Puritan faith (Congregationalism) enjoyed the same favored status that Anglicanism had in the South. The Puritans had emerged as a party within the Church of England during the reign of Queen Elizabeth (1558-1603). It was their aim, as the name implies, to "purify" the Church of England of the vestiges of Catholicism. The Puritans regarded themselves as the true Church of England and, except for a small group known as Separatists, the Puritans had no desire to separate from the Church of England. But the Church of England, on the other hand, had no desire to be purified of its episcopal government and its ritual.

When an impasse was reached between the Puritans and the Church of England, and when Archbishop Laud began persecuting them, the Puritans turned to the New World. They obtained a charter for the Massachusetts Bay Company in 1629, and under the leadership of John Winthrop they began a "great migration" which brought 20,000 Puritans to New England within a decade. They had come to the New World to set up a "holy commonwealth," and the church was the center of community life. There were close ties between church and state in New England, and for many years dissenters were not tolerated. The Puritans were Calvinistic in theology and believed they were a covenant people who would be blessed by God if they were faithful in his service. The Puritans contributed more to colonial America than any other religious group and were the largest denomination at the end of the colonial era.

Tiny Rhode Island was founded by a dissident Puritan, Roger Williams. Williams disagreed with Massachusetts Bay authorities about church-state relations, fled the colony, and established Rhode Island in 1636. He became a Baptist for a short time and helped found the first Baptist church in America. Williams and his Rhode Island colony were unique in allowing a greater degree of religious freedom than was enjoyed anywhere else in the world.

The New England Puritans and Southern Anglicans had been forced to tolerate dissenting churches by the 1700's, and the result was diversity, but not such diversity as was found in the middle colonies. New Netherlands, later to become New York, was founded by the Dutch, and the Dutch

Reformed Church was supported by the government. When the British seized New Netherlands in 1664, it is said that 14 different languages were spoken on Long Island – an indication of the national and religious diversity. Pennsylvania, too, was characterized by great religious diversity. The Quakers were the most influential denomination in Pennsylvania since the colony was founded by William Penn, a Quaker. But as a means of inducing settlers to his colony, Penn offered religious freedom to all who believed in God. There were several persecuted German sects who fled to Pennsylvania – the Mennonites of Lancaster County and the Moravians who made Pennsylvania a center of missionary activity. The Lutherans, too, came to Pennsylvania in large numbers.

The major source of Presbyterian strength in America was the great Scotch-Irish immigration of the 1700's. The Scotch-Irish were Presbyterians whose theology was almost identical to that of the New England Puritans, and at first they settled in New England. But finding that they were not accepted by the Puritans, the Scotch-Irish turned to the frontier areas of Pennsylvania, Virginia and the Carolinas. By 1775 the Presbyterians were scattered through all the colonies and were the second largest denomination in America. Thomas and Alexander Campbell, it may be noted, were part of this Scotch-Irish immigration to America, though they did not come until after 1800.

When the Revolution began in 1775, the five largest denominations in America were Congregationalists (with 658 churches), Presbyterians (543), Baptists (498), Anglicans (480), and Quakers (295). The Catholics (50) and Methodists (37) were far behind the leaders, but they were destined to become major denominations in the nineteenth century.

Two Great Awakenings

The Great Awakening was a renewal of religious interest that swept through the colonies during the 1730's and 1740's. The strong religious motivation that had influenced the planting of many of the colonies had waned by 1700, and this decline in religion was followed, in turn, by the revivals of the Great Awakening. The Awakening began among the Dutch Reformed in New Jersey bout 1726 and soon spread to the Presbyterians. Led by Gilbert Tennant, embraced by several ministers but opposed by others, the revival brought serious divisions to the Presbyterians.

The leading figure in the New England phase of the Great Awakening was Jonathan Edwards. The revival began at Northampton, Massachusetts, in 1734, quickly spread through New England, and reached its climax about 1740. Edwards is best known for his sermon, "Sinners in the Hands of an Angry God," and this is unfortunate, for he had one of the keenest theological minds America has produced. The great English preacher, George Whitefield, made five trips to America, preached from New England to Georgia, and became a unifying influence in the Awakening. In the Southern colonies the revivals continued until the eve of the Revolution and resulted in many converts for the Presbyterian, Baptist and Methodist churches.

The Great Awakening quickened interest in religion, but it had important results beyond this. It encouraged humanitarian and missionary concerns and resulted in the founding of several colleges. And it gave the diverse colonies a sense of oneness they had never had before.

The years after the Revolutionary War, like many postwar periods, saw a marked decline in religion. These years have been called "the lowest ebb tide of vitality in the history of American Christianity." Churches were demoralized in the aftermath of the war, and less than ten percent of the people claimed membership in any denomination. This was the time when deistic works like Thomas Paine's *Age of Reason* were ridiculing Christianity. And, as has often in our history, religious apathy was followed by another period of renewal and revival – the Second Great Awakening.

This Second Awakening began on the Atlantic seaboard, but it reached its height in frontier Kentucky. A Presbyterian revivalist, James McGready, went to Logan County, Kentucky, in 1796, and began the work. The revival quickly spread through Kentucky and Tennessee, as many other revivalists – Presbyterians, Baptists and Methodists – worked together in the awakening with little regard for denominational differences. The revival took new forms in the West. "Sacramental meetings" (occasions when the Lord's Supper would be observed) brought worshipers from afar. They came by horseback, wagon or buggy to spend several days at the revival, and the "camp meeting" was born. These camp meetings became the scenes of strange and emotional "exercises," as worshipers were struck unconscious to awaken praising God or jerked uncontrollably until they professed conversion. The revival spread like a prairie fire across Kentucky through the spring and summer of 1801, and reached its climax in August when thousands of people converged on the Presbyterian meetinghouse at Cane Ridge for a camp meeting that is without parallel in American Christianity. The pastor of the Cane Ridge church at the time was Barton W. Stone, and in the aftermath of the revival, he found himself abandoning his Presbyterian church and beginning a search for New Testament Christianity.

The O'Kelly Movement

But Barton W. Stone was not the first American to envision a purified primitive church. James O'Kelly had seen the same dream a full decade earlier than Stone. O'Kelly (1735-1826) was a North Carolina farmer who became a lay preacher in the Methodist Church during the Revolutionary War. Methodism, at the time, was in its infancy in the New World and still a "society" within the Anglican Church. The first Methodists had appeared in America in the 1760's, and in 1771 John Wesley sent Francis Asbury to the New World as his "general assistant." When the American colonies gained their independence, John Wesley wrote a letter to his disciples in America suggesting that they sever their ties with the Anglican Church and form an independent denomination. Thus the Methodist Episcopal Church was organized at the famous "Christmas Conference" in 1784, and Francis Asbury was elected "superintendent" or bishop.

James O'Kelly was present at the "Christmas Conference" but was not pleased that the Methodists adopted an episcopal form of church government. Later, he charged that "a church was organized *of ministers, by ministers, and for ministers,* with Rev. Francis Asbury at its head." However, O'Kelly accepted an appointment as a "presiding elder" for southern Virginia and served until 1792 with as many as 28 preachers under his supervision. But O'Kelly continued to oppose what he considered Asbury's "autocratic rule" and urged a more democratic government for Methodism. The struggle between O'Kelly and Asbury came to a climax at the General Conference held in Baltimore in 1792. O'Kelly proposed that the Conference should have a veto power over Asbury's appointment of preachers. After a long and bitter debate, the Conference voted to support Asbury. The very next day it received a letter from O'Kelly announcing his withdrawal from the church.

O'Kelly and his supporters met at Piney Grove, Virginia, in August 1793, and drafted a resolution which called on Francis Asbury to call a meeting which would "form a permanent plan for peace and union, taking the Holy Scriptures for our guide." Asbury refused, and the O'Kelly group had no alternative but to organize a new church. They took this step on December 25, 1793, and gave their church the name "Republican Methodist Church." Several former Methodist preachers joined in organizing the new church and within a short time it had 1,000 members. In 1794 the new church agreed that the scriptural plan of church government was to ordain elders over each church, and they agreed to drop the name "Republican Methodist." But what would they call themselves? It was Rice Haggard who suggested the answer – the name "Christian" was given by divine authority and they would wear it to the exclusion of all others.

The new "Christian Church" spread through the Southern and Western states and by 1809 it had a membership of

20,000. Its basic beliefs included the lordship of Christ as the only head of the church, the name Christian to the exclusion of all others, and the Bible as their only creed or rule of faith and practice. Whenever a group adopts such principles as these, it seems that the question of baptism inevitably arises. The question was debated in the O'Kelly movement in 1810, but O'Kelly refused to be convinced that immersion was the only scriptural baptism. The result was division, as those favoring immersion refused to remain in the Christian Church.

The New England Christians

Meanwhile, "Christian churches" began to appear in New England, which were quite similar to those of the O'Kelly movement but which were completely independent of the Southern churches in origin. The O'Kelly movement came out of the Methodist church, and the issue was church government, but the New England Christians were Baptist in background, and the issue was doctrinal – Calvinism. The leaders in the New England restoration were Elias Smith and Abner Jones. Smith was a Baptist preacher who, dissatisfied with Calvinism, came to believe that all theological systems were wrong and that Christians should be guided only by scripture. Abner Jones was also a Baptist preacher and, influenced by Smith's teaching, he organized an independent "Christian Church" at Lyndon, Vermont, in 1801. Six years later there were 14 churches and 12 ministers in the new church.

Elias Smith began publishing the *Herald of Gospel Liberty* in 1808, and the early issues of this journal reveal how the New England Christians and those in the South developed a sense of fellowship with one another. On May 27, 1809, for example, several Christian ministers from Virginia and the Carolinas sent greetings to brethren in New England. And they stated that they rejoiced to know that the New England Christians accepted, as they did, the headship of Christ over the church, the New Testament as the only rule of faith, and the name "Christian." The New Englanders, in turn, returned the greeting. Two years later, Elias Smith attended a conference of Christian preachers in the South. There were discussions about whether the two groups could unite and Smith was given the right hand of fellowship.

The church which resulted from these two early efforts at restoration came to be known as the "Christian Connection" and remained separate from the Stone and Campbell movements. But in 1931 it merged with the Congregationalists to form the Congregational Christian Church, and this new denomination, in turn, merged with the Evangelical and Reformed to produce the United Church of Christ in 1957.

Questions for review and discussion

1. What is meant by an "established church"? What denominations were "established" in colonial America?
2. Who were the Puritans? Where did they settle in America? What were their beliefs?
3. What was the religious pattern in the middle colonies?
4. What effect did the two great awakenings have on the religious history of our country?

Story of the Restoration

5. What were the largest denominations in America at the end of the colonial period?
6. How did the restoration movement led by James O'Kelly originate?
7. Discuss the New England Christians. How were they similar to the O'Kelly movement? How were they different?
8. Identify the following:
   (1) William Stone
   (2) Roger Williams
   (3) Jonathan Edwards
   (4) George Whitefield
   (5) James McGready
   (6) John Winthrop
   (7) Francis Asbury
   (8) "Christmas Conference"
   (9) "Camp meeting"
   (10) Rice Haggard
   (11) Elias Smith
   (12) Christian Connection

Chapter 2
The Stone Movement

"Do you accept the Westminster Confession of Faith as containing the system of doctrine taught in the Bible?" Robert Marshall asked the candidate for ordination.

"I do, as far as I see it consistent with the word of God," was the reply.

These were the words of Barton W. Stone as he stood before the Transylvania Presbytery at Cane Ridge, Kentucky, October 4, 1798, to be ordained into the Presbyterian ministry. Stone had experienced many uncertainties en route to his ordination, and his answer reflected the contrast between his inner misgivings about Calvinistic theology and his resolute faith in the Bible.

Early Life and Ministry

Barton W. Stone (1771-1844) was the son of a well-to-do Maryland planter. After his father died, the family moved to the Virginia frontier in 1779. The revolutionary War was then in progress, and Stone, not yet ten years old, actually witnessed some of the last desperate fighting. The estate of John Stone was divided among his children in 1790, and Barton determined to invest his inheritance in an education at David Caldwell's Academy in North Carolina. The Academy was a one-man college, but it was an excellent school by the standards of that day.

David Caldwell was a Presbyterian minister, and religious influences dominated the life of his Academy. While

Story of the Restoration

Stone was a student there, James McGready, a famous Presbyterian revivalist, visited the school and conducted a revival which resulted in the conversion of most of the student body. Stone was impressed with McGready's preaching, but somehow McGready's Calvinistic emphasis on the wrath of God left him convicted of sin but without hope of mercy. Stone went through a year of inner struggle, wanting to find assurance of salvation, but he saw no ray of hope. He said of McGready, "He left me – without one encouraging word." Later, William Hodge visited Caldwell's school and stressed the love of God in his sermons, and the result was Stone's conversion. Stone's interests turned toward the Presbyterian ministry, and this meant preaching a trial sermon before the Presbytery. Though the subject assigned, "The Trinity," was a difficult one, Stone's sermon was accepted.

However, Stone's struggles with the Trinity had left him with misgivings about Presbyterian theology, and without waiting for his license to preach, he left Caldwell's school for Washington, Georgia. He found a job teaching in a new school operated by a Methodist preacher, Hope Hull. Hull had been present at the Methodist General Conference in 1792 when the Asbury-O'Kelly conflict came to its climax and had voted with O'Kelly. But he had refused to leave the Methodist church with him. It seems likely that through his association with Hull, Stone would have learned of O'Kelly and his break with Methodism.

After he had returned to North Carolina and received his license to preach in 1796, Stone turned to the west – Tennessee and Kentucky. He went through Nashville in 1796 and described it as "a poor little village scarcely worth notice" – its population was then about 300 – then turned northward into Kentucky. He began preaching for two small Presbyterian churches at Cane Ridge and Concord, and two years later in 1798, Stone received a formal call to be ordained. This brought another personal crisis. Stone had serious misgivings about certain points in Presbyterian theology, and as part of the ordination ceremony he was asked the ceremonial question about whether he accepted the Confession of Faith. It was then that Stone responded, "I do, as far as I see it consistent with the word of God."

The Cane Ridge Meeting

The same year that Stone arrived in Kentucky, 1796, James McGready had also come west and had begun preaching in Logan County in southern Kentucky. Logan County was then lawless frontier with more sin than civilization. The following spring (May 1797) an awakening occurred at McGready's Gasper River church. This is a significant date, for it marks the beginning of the Second Great Awakening in the West. The awakening began to spread, and other preachers such as William and John McGee joined McGready in the work. Two noteworthy features of the awakening in southern Kentucky were the intense emotionalism and "exercises" which occurred and the participation of revivalists from different denominations. John McGee, who was a Methodist, wrote Francis Asbury, "Party spirit and narrow faced bigotry are dying fast."

Meanwhile, nearly 200 miles northeast of Logan County, Barton Stone was pastoring his church at Cane Ridge and wrestling with two problems. One was his uncertainty about the Calvinistic theology of his church. Later, Stone recalled that often when he was preaching the doctrine of depravity and human helplessness and then trying to persuade the helpless to repent, his spirit "would be chilled at the contradiction." Stone's second problem was the worsening spiritual apathy. Stone first heard of the revival spreading across southern Kentucky in the fall of 1800, and the next spring he went to Logan County to observe what was happening. The strange "exercises" baffled Stone, and he observed with "critical attention" several acquaintances who were struck down. As a result of what he saw, Stone's "conviction was complete that it was a good work – the work of God."

When Stone returned to Cane Ridge, his preaching began producing the same results that he had witnessed in Logan County – a revival accompanied by intense emotionalism and the "exercises." The spring and early summer of 1801 saw the revival spreading across the bluegrass country of Kentucky as other preachers fanned the flames of revival. The climax of the great awakening in the West occurred at Stone's Cane Ridge church in August of 1801, when a camp meeting was held which is without parallel in American history. A vast throng of people camped in the woods around the log church. Estimates of attendance vary widely, but Stone reported that "military men" on the ground estimated that between 20,000 and 30,000 were present. The revival continued for six days, night and day, without respite. The revival was unprecedented in the hundreds, perhaps even thousands, who succumbed to the "exercises." The victims would fall with a piercing scream, lie unconscious for hours, and awaken to praise God. Richard

McNemar, one of the preachers in the revival, reported that one man kept a tally of those who "fell" and the tally was about 3,000.

The Cane Ridge meeting was unique, too, in the large number of preachers of different denominations who shared in the work. Stone reported, "The Methodist and Baptist preachers aided in the work, and all appeared cordially united in it." Denominational lines were blurred. According to Stone, "All united in prayer – all preached the same things – free salvation urged upon all by faith and repentance." But "free salvation for all" hardly seemed consistent with predestination and a limited atonement, and, as might have been predicted, the revival aroused strong opposition in the Presbyterian Church. Richard McNemar was the first of the revivalists to be charged with heresy. He was called an "Armenian" in 1802, and when the charges came before the Synod of Kentucky in September 1803, five Presbyterian revivalists were present – Robert Marshall, John Dunlavy and John Thompson, along with McNemar and Stone. Even before the Synod could conduct its heresy trial, these five men announced that they were renouncing the authority of the Synod.

The Springfield Presbytery

The revivalists' next step was to organize their own association, which they called the Springfield Presbytery, and prepare a defense of their action. The defense was entitled *An Apology for Renouncing the Jurisdiction of the Synod of Kentucky,* and one section, written by Stone, argued that certain teachings in the Westminster Confession of Faith were contrary to scripture. The Springfield Presbytery was

Story of the Restoration

a short-lived body (if, indeed, it ever was a "live" functioning organization), for within five months of its formation, the five revivalists came to believe that there was no scriptural authority for such an organization and abandoned it.

The document announcing the disbanding of the organization was signed on June 28, 1804 – the now-famous "Last Will and Testament of the Springfield Presbytery." It was a serious document, earnest in spirit, yet written in a satirical style. The following were some of the key items:

We *will*, that this body die, be dissolved, and sink into union with the Body of Christ at large; for there is but one Body, and one Spirit, even as we are called in one hope of our calling. ...

We *will*, that our power of making laws for the government of the church, and executing them by delegated authority, forever cease; that the people may have free course to the Bible, and adopt the law of the Spirit of life in Christ Jesus. ...

We *will,* that the people henceforth take the Bible as the only sure guide to heaven; and as many as are offended with other books, which stand in competition with it, may cast them into the fire if they choose; for it is better to enter into life having one book, than having many to be cast into hell."

Other items in the "Last Will and Testament" were obvious thrusts at the Presbyterians and their treatment of the revivalists. The authors stated that candidates for the ministry should "obtain license to preach from God" and should preach the simple gospel without the "traditions of men" – a thrust at the Confession. They stressed the complete independence of the local church and the right of each church to examine a minister as to his soundness in the faith – an obvious reference to McNemar's heresy trials.

What name was to be worn by the signers of the "Last Will and Testament" if they were no longer Presbyterians? Their desire to take the Bible "as the only sure guide to heaven" suggested an answer, and at the same meeting at which they disbanded the Springfield Presbytery the revivalists agreed to call themselves "Christians." By a coincidence of history, Rice Haggard, who had proposed the name "Christian" to the O'Kelly movement in 1794, was a visitor at the Cane Ridge church exactly a decade later. And it was he who proposed the name "Christian" to the ex-Presbyterians. Shortly after this, Stone began to sign his name "Barton W. Stone, E.C.C.," i.e., Elder in the Church of Christ. However, the churches associated with the Stone movement were usually called "Christian churches." And before the year 1804 had ended, the new reformation included 15 such "Christian churches," seven in Ohio and eight in Kentucky.

Problems and Programs

The Christian Church was confronted with several discouraging problems during its first decade of existence. First, there were defections to the Shakers. The Shakers were a strange sect who demanded complete celibacy and a communitarian way of life for all their members. Newspaper accounts of the "exercises" accompanying the western revival attracted the Shakers' attention, and they dispatched three missionaries to Kentucky early in 1805. Within less than a year, four Christian preachers had accepted Shakerism, including two of the signers of the "Last Will and

Testament" – Richard McNemar and John Dunlavy. McNemar was destined to be the outstanding Shaker leader in the West for the next 30 years. The defections seemed a very serious loss at the time; but historians have noted that those attracted by Shakerism might have been so fanatical as to cause trouble for Stone later, and their leaving might have been a blessing in disguise.

The question of baptism was raised in the Stone movement in 1807. When it was decided that immersion would be practiced, Stone immersed David Purviance, and Purviance, in turn, immersed Reuben Dooley. Purviance and Dooley were among the first preachers who had joined the movement after the Christian Church was launched. Immersion was soon widely practiced among the Christians; and even though it was not made a test of fellowship, Stone could write in 1826, "There is not one in five hundred among us who has not been immersed."

Another practice which appeared quite early among the Christians was the organization of "conferences" among the preachers. The purpose of these conferences was fellowship and discussion, not to "meddle in the government of the churches," as Stone put it. Baptism and the atonement were discussed at one of these conferences in 1811, and Robert Marshall and John Thompson revealed that they still held orthodox Presbyterian views on the subjects. Later in the year, they renounced the Christian Church and returned to the Presbyterians. Ironically, they had been among the five signers of the "Last Will and Testament," and thus two of the five had accepted Shakerism and two had returned to Presbyterianism. No wonder Stone later reminisced about his discouragement, "Of all the five of us that left the Presbyterians, I only was left, and they sought my life."

But all was not discouragement. The work grew despite problems, and by 1807 Stone could count 24 churches in four states – Kentucky, Ohio, Indiana and Tennessee. The following year witnessed a camp meeting with 47 preachers and "very great crowds" present. One evidence of the vitality of the movement is the number of preachers who joined Stone in preaching a return to a non-creedal New Testament Christianity. Some of these preachers had earlier been associated with James O'Kelly in Virginia and the Carolinas. But when they came to the West and discovered that Stone was preaching the same basic principles they already accepted, they added their strength to the Christian churches in the West. Rice Haggard, who suggested the name "Christian" to Stone, is one example, but there were many others – David Haggard, Clement Nance, James Read and John O'Kane among them.

There were others who came into the Stone movement by way of their own independent study of the Scripture and resolution to follow it to the exclusion of every creed. John Mulkey was such a man. While preaching for a Baptist Church near Tompkinsville, Kentucky in 1809, Mulkey came to believe that the major tenets of Calvinism were unscriptural. He announced to his congregation that he was going to take his stand upon the Bible alone and invited them to join him. A great many did and Mulkey's church soon became associated with the Christians and became a radiating point for the restoration plea in that part of Kentucky.

Story of the Restoration

And all the while, Stone was busy converting many, inspiring them to preach, and training others at schools which he operated at Lexington (1815-1819) and Georgetown (1819-1834). Stone began a journal, the *Christian Messenger*, in 1826, and it served as a unifying force among the Christians. It is estimated that by 1832 (when the two major branches of the Restoration Movement were united) the Stone movement had 10,000 members in Kentucky, perhaps half that number in Ohio, and others scattered across Tennessee, Alabama, Indiana, Illinois and Missouri. As Stone described it, the plea to restore the primitive faith had "spread like fire in dry stubble."

Questions for review and discussion

1. Trace Stone's early life and religious experiences up to the time of his ordination as a Presbyterian minister.
2. Describe the Cane Ridge meeting.
3. Why did some Presbyterians oppose the revivals?
4. What were the main themes in the "Last Will and Testament of the Springfield Presbytery"?
5. What were some of the problems the Stone movement faced during its early years?
6. Were there any ties between the Stone movement and the earlier O'Kelly movement?
7. How was each of the following related to the Stone movement?
   (1) Logan County, KY
   (2) James McGready
   (3) David Caldwell

Bill Humble, PhD.

(4) Richard McNemar
(5) Rice Haggard
(6) John Mulkey
(7) Shakers
(8) Christian Messenger
(9) Hope Hull

Chapter 3
The Campbell Movement

"Where the Scriptures speak, we speak; and where the Scriptures are silent, we are silent."

These are the words of Thomas Campbell, and they were first spoken in 1809 as he stood before a small group known as the "Christian Association of Washington." Two years earlier, Campbell had come to the United States from Ireland, little realizing that he would soon break with his denomination and play a formative role in the Restoration Movement. Who was this man? And what chain of events had led him to this hour?

Thomas Campbell

Thomas Campbell (1763-1854) had been a faithful minister in the Seceder Presbyterian Church in Ireland before his migration to the United States in 1807. Campbell was Scotch-Irish and had been reared in the Church of England, but he became dissatisfied with its formalism and joined the Seceder Presbyterians. Campbell had been educated at the University of Glasgow (1783-1786) and had also received his theological training in Scotland. By 1791 he was a Presbyterian minister, and from that date until his migration to America, Campbell served Seceder churches and operated private academies in Ireland (the last nine years at Rich Hill, 30 miles southwest of Belfast).

Yet even in Ireland, Thomas Campbell was exposed to influences which prepared him for the role he would later play in the American restoration. For example, there was his philosophical background. He has studied John Locke's famous works, *Letters Concerning Toleration* and *The Reasonableness of Christianity*, and the Scottish "common sense" philosophy which followed Locke. Locke had scorned the divisions which had fragmented Christendom, and advocated a simple nonsectarian Christianity which could be achieved, he thought, by returning to a few essential New Testament doctrines. Thomas Campbell was also familiar with Independent (or Congregational) churches in Scotland and Ireland, which had resulted from the work of men like John Glas, Robert Sandeman and the Haldane brothers. The Seceder Presbyterians were narrow and dogmatic, and when Thomas Campbell attended the Independent church at Rich Hill, he saw a different spirit – appeals for wider Christian fellowship, a deeper piety, and a return to the simple practices of early Christians. And finally, distressed that his own Seceder denomination was split into several hostile sects, Thomas Campbell had played the role of peacemaker in 1805 and had led an effort to unite the Seceder factions. Though the effort failed, Campbell's vision of a wider Christian fellowship was not lost.

When Thomas Campbell was 45, he left his family and native Ireland behind and migrated to America. By a happy coincidence the Synod of his Seceder Presbyterian Church was meeting in Philadelphia when he landed there on May 13, 1807. He presented his credentials and was assigned to the Chartiers Presbytery in southwest Pennsylvania. Soon Campbell was a respected minister in Washington, Pennsylvania. Yet within less than six months of his arrival in America, charges were brought against him in the Chartiers

Presbytery, and after a series of church trials which dragged on for a year, he renounced his church and its jurisdiction.

What caused Thomas Campbell's break with the Presbyterian Church? The oft repeated story is that Thomas Campbell was visiting a frontier settlement, invited non-Seceder Presbyterians to commune with the Seceders, and was quickly charged with violating the strict rules of his denomination. While it is true that Campbell longed for a wider circle of christian fellowship, there were more serious differences between him and his denomination. The charges which were brought against Campbell in the Chartiers Presbytery included an accusation that he believed there was no divine authority for confessions of faith. And other charges related to the nature of faith, the right of laymen to exhort when no ordained clergyman was present, and the right of Seceder Presbyterians to hear ministers of other denominations.

The Chartiers Presbytery suspended Campbell from the ministry, and he, in turn, appealed his case to the highest authority in his denomination, the Synod. Meeting in May 1808, the Synod spent nearly a week considering the charges against him. The Synod's verdict was that Thomas Campbell had departed from some of the doctrines and practices of his denomination, and they sentenced him to be "rebuked and admonished" – a surprisingly mild punishment under the circumstances. After the public rebuke, Campbell was allowed to preach in Philadelphia for two months. But when he returned to his home in Washington, the Chartiers Presbytery made it clear that Campbell was no longer welcome in their midst, and on September 13,

1808, he "declined the authority" of the Presbytery, thereby withdrawing from the Presbyterian Church.

Christian Association of Washington

But Thomas Campbell did not quit preaching. Nor did he attempt to organize a new church. Instead, he continued to preach to his friends and sympathizers whenever he had an opportunity, and he stressed the themes that had become so important to him – the sinfulness of sectarian divisions, the need for a wider circle of Christian fellowship, and the importance of following the Scripture rather than creeds or confessions of faith.

Nearly a year after Campbell's withdrawal from the Presbyterians, he and his friends decided to form an organization to "give more definiteness" to their movement for wider fellowship among Christians. And so, on August 17, 1809, they organized the "Christian Association of Washington." The Christian Association was never intended to be a church. It did not function like a church, for it met only semi-annually. Then what was the purpose of the Association? According to its own statement of purpose, it was a group of "voluntary advocates for church reformation ... formed for the sole purpose of promoting simple evangelical Christianity." The Association planned to support ministers, not "only such as reduce to practice that simple original form of Christianity, expressly exhibited from the sacred page."

Thomas Campbell was authorized to prepare a formal statement explaining the purposes of the Christian Association, and the result was the *Declaration and Address* – the most significant historical document in the history of the

Restoration Movement in America. (The *Declaration and Address* will be studied in some detail in the next chapter.) When the Christian Association met on September 7, 1809, to consider the *Declaration and Address,* Thomas Campbell addressed the group, and it was in this speech that he summarized the Association's purposes in the famous plea, "We speak where the Bible speaks, and we are silent where the Bible is silent." The Christian Association adopted the *Declaration and Address* and authorized its publication.

Alexander Campbell

Just a few weeks after writing the *Declaration and Address,* Thomas Campbell welcomed his family to America. If the 30 months of separation had changed the course of Thomas Campbell's life, they had been eventful, too, for the family. A year earlier, in 1808, they had attempted the voyage to America but had been shipwrecked on an island off the coast of Scotland. It was on the night of the shipwreck, while anxiously awaiting rescue, that Thomas Campbell's 20 year old son, Alexander, made a decision which he had often considered – to devote his life to the ministry. Following the shipwreck, it was too late in the year to attempt the voyage to America again, and the Campbell family went to Glasgow and lived there for ten months. The shipwreck may have bee a "blessing in disguise," at least for Alexander, for it gave him an opportunity to attend the University of Glasgow for one term.

The year that Alexander Campbell (1788-1866) spent at the university was destined to bring important influences to bear on his life. First, it gave him an opportunity to broaden his earlier education, and even more important, it brought him in contact with a religious movement in Scotland which acquainted him with the plea to return to primitive Christianity. The leaders of this Scottish restoration movement were two brothers, Robert and James Alexander Haldane. Wealthy members of the Church of Scotland, they had begun a movement in the 1790's for an evangelical revival and greater missionary zeal in the Church of Scotland. Discouraged at the lack of response, they withdrew from the Church of Scotland in 1799 and began establishing "independent" churches. They began practicing congregational independence and the weekly observance of the Lord's Supper, and soon they were calling for a restoration of New Testament practices. James Haldane wrote in 1805, "All Christians are bound to observe the universal and approved practices of the first churches recorded in Scripture" – a statement whose restorationist thrust is obvious. By 1807 the Haldanes had become convinced that the New Testament churches did not sprinkle infants and were practicing immersion. The Haldanes established many churches in Scotland, England and Ireland; and even in America "churches of Christ" were begun with roots going back to the Haldane movement.

Alexander Campbell became acquainted with the Haldane movement through Greville Ewing, former minister of the Church of Scotland who was operating a seminary for the Haldanes in Glasgow. Ewing befriended the Campbell family after their shipwreck, and introduced Alexander to the Haldanes and their program for restoring New Testament Christianity. The months of association with the Haldane movement gradually weakened Alexander Campbell's loyalty to his Seceder Presbyterian Church, and near the end of his Glasgow residence, he refused to participate in a Seceder communion service. Never again would he be a member of the Presbyterian Church. Later, as Campbell recalled his year in Glasgow, he reminisced, "My faith in creeds and confessions of human device was considerable shaken while in Scotland, and I commenced my career in this country under the conviction that nothing that was not as old as the New Testament should be made an article of faith ... or a term of communion amongst Christians."

When Alexander Campbell landed in the United States on September 29, 1809, he was a young man without a church, but with a mission – to give his life to preaching simple New Testament Christianity. As the family traveled across Pennsylvania en route to a reunion with their father, Alexander must have had mixed emotions: joy at the thought of seeing his father again, but apprehension about how his father would react to his new religious views. And meanwhile, Thomas Campbell must have had similar apprehensions, for he had not burdened his family with the unpleasant news that he had renounced the Presbyterian Church. Separated by an ocean, father and son had begun the same search for primitive Christianity. Legend has it that when Thomas Campbell met his family somewhere in central Pennsylvania, he carried the galley proofs of the *Declaration and Address* in his saddlebags. Whether this is true of not, Alexander Campbell soon read the document and knew that he would give his life to its principles. It had been the mission of the father to pen this bold call for a restoration of New Testament Christianity, and it would now be the mission of the son to seek its accomplishment.

Bill Humble, PhD.

The Brush Run Church

Alexander Campbell preached his first sermon on July 15, 1810, after several months of intensive preparatory study. Without license or authority from any church, he continued to preach and within a year he had delivered more than a hundred sermons. (The outlines of many of these sermons were discovered only recently in Campbell family papers which had been carried to Australia.) Meanwhile, Thomas Campbell had asked to be accepted as a minister in the main Presbyterian Church in the United States, but he had already broken with too many points of Presbyterianism for this overture to have any chance of success. Rebuffed and now, more than ever, a man without a church, Thomas Campbell saw that the only alternative was to transform the Christian Association of Washington into a church.

Thus the Brush Run Church was organized on May 4, 1811, nearly three years after Thomas Campbell's break with the Presbyterians. the little church began with 30 members, one elder (Thomas Campbell) and four deacons. The principle which underlay the formation of the Brush Run Church was the autonomy of each local community of Christians, their right to organize themselves as a church without appealing to any ecclesiastical structure for authority and without subscribing to any creed other than the Bible. Two practices which were to become distinctive in the Restoration Movement were accepted by the Brush Run Church from the beginning – the weekly observance of the Lord's Supper and immersion. There were three who wanted to be members of the new church who had never been baptized, either by sprinkling or immersion, and they asked

Story of the Restoration

Thomas Campbell to immerse them. He consented, even though he himself had never been immersed and still believed that it was unnecessary to "rebaptize" anyone who had been sprinkled in infancy.

The Campbells had crossed their Rubicon in organizing the Brush Run Church, for instead of working as an "association" within the fellowship of older churches, they had now constituted themselves as a separate church. But their mission was unchanged. That mission, as expressed in the *Declaration and Address,* was to return to the "simple original form of Christianity" by rejecting everything for which they could not produce a "Thus saith the Lord."

Questions for Review and Discussion

1. What early influences prepared Thomas Campbell for the role of religious reformer?
2. Why did Thomas Campbell break with the Seceder Presbyterian Church"
3. What was the nature of the Christian Association of Washington?
4. What is meant by Thomas Campbell's famous statement, "We speak where the Bible speaks and are silent where it is silent"?
5. What caused Alexander Campbell to break with the Presbyterian Church?
6. Why was the Brush Run Church organized? How was it similar to a church of Christ of today?
7. What was unusual about the reunion of Thomas and Alexander Campbell in America?
8. Identify the following

Bill Humble, PhD.

(1) Declaration and Address
(2) Chartiers Presbytery
(3) Haldane brothers
(4) Greville Ewing
(5) University of Glasgow
(6) John Locke

Chapter 4
The Restoration Principle

Thomas Campbell's *Declaration and Address* has been described by William Warren Sweet as one of the greatest religious documents ever produced in America. The importance of this document lies in its formulation of the restoration principle. There is no other statement by an early restoration leader that is as thorough or detailed in its treatment of the restoration principle. And thus if we are to understand the restoration principle as the pioneers of the movement understood it, we must know something of the contents of the *Declaration and Address* (a 56 page pamphlet when it first came from the press in 1809).

Unity through restoration

Thomas Campbell had long been distressed at the tragic divisions within Christendom. Even in Ireland he had worked to bring his fragmented denomination back together. And in America, his concern for Christian unity had played a part in the troubles which led him to renounce the Seceders. Thus it is not surprising that one of the recurring themes in the *Declaration and Address* is the sin of religious division. Campbell wrote, "The Church of Christ upon earth is essentially, intentionally, and constitutionally one." Except for the plea, "Let us speak where the Bible speaks and be silent where it is silent," this is probably the most significant sentence that Campbell ever penned. The word "essentially" means that in its very essence or nature the true church possesses unity. "Intentionally" means that this oneness or unity is according to divine design. And "constitutionally" means that the church's constitution – the New Testament – makes this unity possible. This statement about the oneness of the church was one of 13 propositions in which Campbell himself summarized all the leading ideas of the *Declaration and Address.* Another said:

Division among the Christians is a horrid evil, fraught with many evils. It is antichristian, as it destroys the visible unity of the body of Christ; as if he were divided against himself, excluding and excommunicating a part of himself. It is antiscriptural, as being strictly prohibited by his sovereign authority; a direct violation of his express command. It is antinatural, as it excites Christians to condemn, to hate, and oppose one another.... In a word, it is productive of confusion and of every evil work.

It is easy to denounce division as wrong but it is not so easy to propose a means of achieving unity. For Thomas Campbell, the road to religious unity lay in a return to the patterns of New Testament Christianity. Influenced by John Locke, Campbell believed that the essentials of Christianity were so clearly revealed in the New Testament that everyone should be willing to accept them. If unity was to be achieved, "nothing ought to be inculcated upon Christians as articles of faith; nor required of them as terms of communion ... but what is expressly enjoined by the authority of our Lord Jesus Christ and his apostles upon the New Testament church; either in express terms or by approved precedent." By "express term" Campbell meant a direct command, and by "approved precedent" he meant New Testament examples. Campbell also believed that the New

Testament taught by inference, but he did not believe that truths known only by inference should be bound on the consciences of others. Here, then, is one of the key concepts in Thomas Campbell's formulation of the restoration principle – whatever is not expressly authorized in the New Testament either by command or example cannot be made a test of fellowship. Here is the way Campbell put it, "Nothing ought to be received into the faith or worship of the church, or be made a term of communion among Christians, that is not as old as the New Testament."

Thomas Campbell believed that the New Testament was a divine pattern for what God expected the church to be in every age. He described the New Testament as "a perfect constitution for the worship, discipline, and government of the New Testament church" and a perfect rule of faith and practice for its members, just as the Old Testament had been for the Old Testament community. (Incidentally, this distinction between Old and New Testaments was a novel idea in Campbell's day, and later, Alexander Campbell made it the theme of his famous "Sermon on the Law.") Campbell often used such expressions as "perfect constitution," "perfect model" and "original standard" to describe the New Testament's authority over the church.

The concepts of unity and restoration were complementary in the thought of Thomas Campbell. He believed that if all denominations would accept the New Testament as the divine constitution for the church and voluntarily abandon any practice not expressly authorized in the New Testament, denominational lines would disappear – and Christian unity would be achieved. After he had called the New

Testament a "perfect model" for the church, Campbell pleaded:

Let us do as we are there expressly told *they* did, say as *they* said; that is, profess and practice as therein expressly enjoined by precept and precedent, in every possible instance, after *their* approved example; and in so doing we shall realize and exhibit all that unity and uniformity that the primitive church possessed.

Thus, there are two basic ideas in Campbell's plea for restoration: (1) the New Testament is a divine constitution for the church, and the church has no right to practice anything that is not expressly authorized in this constitution; (2) a return to the faith and practice of the New Testament would end the differences among denominations and restore the essential oneness of Christ's church.

The *Declaration and Address* was a bold and visionary statement or principle. It was a program for the future. But it did not attempt to apply the restoration principle to immediate problems; nor did it attempt to specify what would be practiced, and what abandoned, in the restored church. For example, what about baptism? Historically, it seems that whenever the restoration of the primitive church has been proposed, the question of baptism is soon raised. But Thomas Campbell did not even mention baptism in the *Declaration and Address*. He had just broken with the Presbyterian Church, and he still assumed without question that the members of all denominations were Christians. And he believed that all these Christians accepted the truths that were essential to a restored and united church. But as Thomas Campbell soon discovered, it was not this simple. He was soon asked, "If we can practice only what is expressly authorized in the New Testament, how can we continue to sprinkle infants?" And when questions like this began to be raised, the problem of applying the restoration principle came into focus.

The Restoration Principle in Practice

The task of applying the restoration concept to the complex problems of everyday church life was to become the major work of Alexander Campbell. Particularly during the years when he edited the *Christian Baptist* (1823-1830), the younger Campbell undertook the task of measuring all contemporary religious practices by the New Testament pattern. He declared, "I contend that the constitution of the church and its laws are found explicitly declared in the New Testament." Beginning in 1825 Campbell wrote a series of 30 articles in the *Christian Baptist* entitled "A Restoration of the Ancient Order of Things." And the special task of these articles was to measure the practices of Protestantism by the New Testament pattern.

Campbell began the series by distinguishing between "reformation" and "restoration." He acknowledged that many reformations had been attempted and that the reformers had been great benefactors of mankind. But whereas human systems could be reformed, Campbell denied that it was proper to speak of reforming Christianity. It was perfect when it began, and any attempt to reform it would be as futile as an attempt to create a new sun. What was needed, Campbell insisted, was "a restoration of the ancient order of things." And this would be achieved by bringing the church "up to the standard of the New Testament." If this could be done, the result would be a golden age for Christianity – the millennium.

Church membership. When Campbell applied the restoration principle to the question, "How does one become a citizen in Christ's kingdom?" he concluded that faith and immersion were the essential requirements. Thomas Campbell's *Declaration and Address* had defined church membership in terms of faith in Christ and obedience to him, but it had made no effort to spell out what was included in obedience. Very soon, Alexander sensed that infant sprinkling was not "expressly enjoined" in the New Testament, and after intensive study he accepted immersion. (More about this in the next lesson.) Thereafter, Campbell insisted that immersion was essential in a restored church. He often used the naturalization analogy to illustrate how men become citizens of Christ's kingdom (a result, perhaps, of his being a naturalized citizen of the United States). How did the apostles receive citizens into Christ's kingdom? They demanded that men acknowledge the King's supremacy by confessing him as the Son of God and express their allegiance in "an act of naturalization" – baptism. And this was the way it had to be done in a restored church.

After the Campbells began practicing immersion, the first goal of the *Declaration and Address* – the unity of all Christians – began to recede into the background. Unity through a return to primitive Christianity had been an appealing plea, but it simply did not work out in practice. Most churches did not accept immersion; and when the Campbells concluded that immersion was essential in a restored church, they were saying, in effect, that here was a biblical truth that Presbyterians, Methodists and many others would have to accept before the oneness of Christ's church could be achieved. But they have refused to accept it. So the goals of unity and restoration, complementary in theory, proved to be antagonistic in practice. Thus the Restoration Movement has faced an unhappy dilemma. It has longed for oneness with all fellow believers in Christ, but it has not been willing to turn aside from the quest for New Testament Christianity in order to achieve that oneness.

Worship. Another excellent example of Campbell's methodology in applying the restoration principle to the concrete problems of Christian duty is found in an article dealing with Christian worship. The American churches were worshiping God in a bewildering array of ways; but Campbell insisted that there were certain divinely authorized acts of public worship that must be practiced in the Christian assembly. Campbell's argument was simple – either there is a divinely authorized pattern of worship, or there is not. If there is not, it would follow that there are no limitations whatever on worship. Anything could be done in the name of worship. Campbell concluded, "Those, then, who contend that there is no divinely authorized order of Christian worship in Christian assemblies, do at the same time, and must inevitable maintain, that there is *no disorder, no error, no innovation, no transgression in the worship of the Christian church – no, nor ever can be."* After establishing this principle, Campbell devoted many articles to discussing the proper acts in public Christian assembly – the weekly observance of the Lord's Supper, singing, prayer and teaching.

Church organization. When Campbell applied the restoration principle to church government, he concluded that the New Testament did not authorize any organization but the local church; and on this basis he denounced Baptist associations, Presbyterian presbyteries and synods, and all episcopal systems. he believed that the New Testament pattern required that each local church be independent and that it be under the oversight of elders (bishops) and served by deacons. Campbell also believed that the common distinction between clergy and laity had no foundation in Scripture, and he was especially caustic in his attacks on the clergy. He called them a "Protestant priesthood" and charged that their creeds and theological jargon stood between the people and the simple faith of the first disciples.

Problems in application

It is easy to state the restoration principle – the church in every age should be as nearly like the New Testament church as possible. It is not so easy to determine what the New Testament requires in each situation. The church must ask, What is universally obligatory in the New Testament pattern? And what may be dismissed as a part of the culture of the ancient world and not binding upon the church in every age? This is a problem of Biblical interpretation – a hermeneutical problem – and the answers are not always easy.

The early restorers faced this problem just as we do. Campbell was often asked why certain New Testament practices were no longer required. The holy kiss? Observing the Lord's Supper at night? Foot washing? Why were these not required in a restored church? Campbell's rationale for dealing with New Testament examples was to study each one in its context and attempt to determine whether it was a common practice which seemed to be required of all the churches, or whether it was a "circumstantial" that was not a part of God's pattern. Campbell's treatment of the community of goods at Jerusalem illustrates his method. He compared the Jerusalem church with other New Testament congregations and concluded that there was no reason to believe that all churches were required to have all things common. But there were others who did not agree with Campbell. Sidney Rigden believed that Jerusalem's community of goods was a model which later churches were bound to follow, and he introduced the practice at Kirtland, Ohio. Later, when Campbell opposed him, Ridden defected to the Mormons and was a rival of Brigham Young for leadership after Joseph Smith's death.

Another problem in applying the restoration principle lay in the silence of the Scripture. Thomas Campbell's *Declaration and Address* had stated that nothing should be admitted into the faith or worship of the church unless it was expressly taught in the New Testament. But did this mean that whatever was not mentioned in the New Testament was forbidden? In 1830 Campbell and Barton Stone disagreed about communing with the unimmersed. Stone was in favor of it, while Campbell was opposed. Stone argued that there was nothing in the Scripture "to forbid me to commune with unbaptized persons." Thus Stone was using the silence of the Scripture to allow a practice. But Campbell responded, "It is not enough to say there is no command against it. Is there no command for it? If there be not a command or precedent for it, we can easily find one against it. Because whatever is not commanded by the Lord is human." Campbell saw the silence of the Scripture as saying, "No, you have no authority to do it." Later, Campbell admitted that expedients like church buildings were necessary. But when instrumental music began to be introduced into the churches, the silence of the Scripture became a serious issue in restoration thought.

Summary

The basic concepts that underlie the restoration principle might be summarized as follows:

(1) The Bible is the inspired Word of God and the final authority for God's people.

(2) The New Testament is a divine pattern or constitution for the church of Christ.

(3) Whenever this pattern is followed, the church will be restored just as it was in the New Testament era.

(4) A chain of true churches stretching back through the centuries is not essential to our being the true church. The only essential is the New Testament. For wherever it is followed, the churches will be like those of the apostolic age.

(5) The churches which follow the New Testament pattern will have the same worship, organization, etc., and will, therefore, be one.

Questions for review and discussion

1. What did the *Declaration and Address* say about Christian unity?
2. Discuss Thomas Campbell's belief that the New Testament is a "perfect constitution" for the church. Do you agree with Campbell? Could one believe in restoring New Testament Christianity

if he did not accept such a view of the New Testament?
3. How were the themes of unity and restoration related in the *Declaration and Address?*
4. How did Alexander Campbell apply the restoration principle to the following questions: How does one become a member of the church? How should the church worship? How is the church organized?
5. What are some of the problems in applying the restoration principle?
6. How did Stone and Campbell differ about the silence of the Scripture in 1830?
7. Summarize the basic principles that underlie the restoration principle.

Chapter 5
Reformers among the Baptists

The question of immersion

The question of baptism was raised very soon after the Campbells accepted the restoration principle. When Thomas Campbell presented the *Declaration and Address* to the Christian Association of Washington in 1809, Andrew Munro objected that if they practiced only what was "expressly enjoined" in the New Testament, they could not sprinkle infants. Thomas Campbell apparently brushed the question aside, but it continued to be raised. When Alexander Campbell was discussing the restoration principle with a Presbyterian minister named Riddle, he was told that however plausible the principle sounded, it would lead him to become a Baptist. Campbell was "mortified" that he could not produce either a New Testament command or example for infant baptism, and he spent nearly a year reading treatises in favor of the practice. The result, he reported, was "indignation at their assumptions and fallacious reasonings," and he turned to a study of the Greek New Testament but found nothing to allay his doubts.

When Alexander Campbell approached his father about baptism, Thomas admitted that there was "neither express terms not express precedent" in the New Testament for sprinkling infants. But he opposed "rebaptism" and insisted that it was unnecessary for Christians to "unchurch" themselves and put off Christ just to be able to make a new profession in immersion. For a time Alexander yielded to his father's views; but after his marriage to Margaret Brown and the birth of their first child in 1812, he studied the question anew. He concluded that sprinkling was not New Testament baptism and that he "was then, in point of fact, an unbaptized person" and could not conscientiously preach to others what he himself had not obeyed. Thus, on June 12, 1812, Alexander Campbell and seven others, including his father, were immersed by Matthias Luse, a Baptist minister. It is noteworthy that Alexander refused to submit to the usual Baptist examination as to whether he was a proper candidate for baptism. Instead, he insisted that baptism should follow a simple confession of faith in Christ. It is noteworthy, too, that the role of leadership in the movement fell increasingly on Alexander Campbell after his decision to be immersed. Henceforth, Thomas Campbell would often be following his son.

If the Campbells' immersion moved them further away from the Presbyterians, it brought them closer to the Baptists. Alexander attended the annual meeting of the Redstone Baptism Association in 1812, but as yet he had no intention of uniting with the Baptists. He disliked what he had seen of Baptist preachers and regarded them as "little men in a big office." But after the Baptists had made several overtures, the Campbells finally consented to unite the Brush Run Church with the Redstone Association in the fall of 1813. But they made it clear that they were not typical Baptists, for they submitted a lengthy written statement saying they would unite with the Association provided they would be free to teach whatever they "learned from the Holy Scriptures regardless of any human creed."

Bill Humble, PhD.

Non-Baptist leaven

The Campbells were destined to spend 17 years (1813-1830) among the Baptists. However, the union was always an uneasy one, for there were Baptist leaders who sensed from the beginning that the Campbells were spreading non-Baptist leaven through the Baptist lump. There were three major avenues that Alexander Campbell used in pleading for reformation among the Baptists: sermons, debates, and a monthly journal.

(1) *Sermons.* The union of the Brush Run Church with the Redstone Association opened many Baptist pulpits to Alexander Campbell. He soon became a popular preacher among Baptist circles, but his sermons sometimes reflected important differences between him and the Baptists. The best illustration of this is the famous "Sermon on the Law" delivered at the annual meeting of the Redstone Association on August 30, 1816. The sermon emphasized the distinction between the law of Moses and the gospel of Christ and stressed the Christian's emancipation from the old covenant. These ideas are now so familiar that they hardly seem novel, but the "Sermon on the Law" seemed so non-Baptist in 1816 that it aroused bitter opposition within the Redstone Association.

(2) *Debates.* Twice, Campbell defended Baptist views in debates with Presbyterians. The first of these debates was with John Walker and was held in Mount Pleasant, Ohio, in 1820. Influenced by his father, Campbell was at first reluctant to engage in such a controversy; but once the debate was under way, Campbell quickly discovered unique powers as a controversialist. He realized, too, that public interest in such debates made them an excellent

means of spreading the restoration plea. The subject of the Walker debate was baptism, and by emphasizing the law-gospel distinction which he had presented in the "Sermon on the Law" Campbell won an easy victory over Walker. But since it was a Baptist victory won with non-Baptist arguments, the Baptists hardly knew whether to laud Campbell or feel apprehensive about the future.

Campbell's second debate was held at Washington, Kentucky, in 1823, and his opponent was W. L. Maccalla. Campbell again argued against infant sprinkling by stressing the difference between the old and new covenants. And discussing the design of baptism, he argued for the first time that baptism brings the promise of the forgiveness of sins. Despite the obvious differences between Campbell and Baptist doctrine, Kentucky Baptists were pleased at the outcome of the Maccalla debate, and Campbell soon had many followers in the state. The Walker and Maccalla debates were both published, and wherever read, they spread Campbell's influence.

(3) *Christian Baptist*. Only a few months before the Maccalla debate, Campbell had begun publishing a monthly journal, the *Christian Baptist,* which was soon widely read in Kentucky, Virginia, Ohio and elsewhere. The *Christian Baptist's* theme was "a restoration of the ancient order of things," and Campbell attempted to judge the faith and practices of Protestantism by the principles which his father had formulated in the *Declaration and Address*. The appeal for the unity of all Christians is found in the *Christian Baptist,* but the real emphasis was on measuring everything by the New Testament and rejecting whatever it did not specifically authorize. The *Christian Baptist* was strong-

ly iconoclastic in spirit; and the three "idols" of Protestantism which it sought to overthrow were the clergy, creeds and organizations. The clergy was an "avaricious priesthood." Creeds shackled the minds of the masses and stood between them and the Scripture. And such organizations as associations, synods and missionary societies were unscriptural and "robbed the church of its glory." Robert Semple, a prominent Virginia Baptist, probably reflected the feelings of many when he denounced the *Christian Baptist* as "more mischievous" than any other journal that he had ever read. But the *Christian Baptist,* more than any other medium, spread Campbell's non-Baptist leaven.

Walter Scott

Sometime during the winter of 1821-1822, Alexander Campbell became acquainted with a young Scotsman named Walter Scott (1796-1861), and in the years ahead Scott was to become Campbell's closest fellow worker in the Restoration Movement. Educated at the University of Edinburgh, Scott had come to the United States in 1818 and had made his way to Pittsburgh a year later. He began teaching in a school in Pittsburgh operated by George Forrester. But Forrester was also the preacher for a small church associated with the Haldane movement, and through Forrester Scott learned of the restoration concept and was immersed. Thus, when Scott first met Campbell two years later, he was already prepared to join Campbell in the work of restoration. When Campbell began his paper in 1823, it was Scott who suggested the name *Christian Baptist* and who wrote frequent articles.

Story of the Restoration

Walter Scott made his greatest contribution to the Restoration Movement as an evangelist of the Mahoning Association, and it was Campbell who persuaded him to undertake this work. By 1823 Campbell's critics in the Redstone Association were bent on excommunicating him, and to thwart their plans Campbell became a member of the Mahoning Baptist Association, located in the "Western Reserve" of Ohio. The churches of the Mahoning Association had been more receptive to Campbell's ideas, and several of them had discarded their creed and resolved to follow only the Bible. But despite this, the Mahoning churches were not growing, and in 1826 the 16 churches showed a net loss in membership, even though the population of the area was multiplying. It was obvious that something was wrong, and in 1827 the association resolved to employ an evangelist to work among the churches. Walter Scott had accompanied Campbell to the association meeting that year, and at Campbell's suggestion he was selected as the evangelist.

Several years earlier, Scott had read a tract teaching that baptism is for the remission of sins. The tract had been written by Henry Errett, an elder in a Haldanean "church of Christ" in New York. The idea had made a deep impression on Scott, and when he became Mahoning evangelist he saw an opportunity to put it into practice. Faith, repentance, baptism, the remission of sins and the gift of the Holy Spirit – this was the "gospel restored" in Scott's preaching. The result was a great revival among the Mahoning churches, but a different kind of revival from those at Cane Ridge and elsewhere in the West. There was none of the emotionalism, no exercises, no continuous camp meetings. Scott preached that anyone could believe the New Testament testimony that Jesus was the Messiah, and upon this faith he should be immersed for the remission of sins. And hundreds responded. When Alexander Campbell heard of the revival sweeping the Mahoning churches, he was concerned and sent his father to observe the work. After seeing, Thomas Campbell wrote that even though they had understood the gospel correctly for a number of years, it was now being put into practice for the first time. As a result of the revival the total membership of the Mahoning churches was more than doubled within one year, and by 1830 the association had been so transformed that it dissolved itself out of existence.

Walter Scott's proclamation of "baptism for the remission of sins" supplied the Campbell movement with an essential which it had previously lacked – a dynamic and successful evangelism. It was an evangelism which emphasized reason rather than emotion, the belief of the New Testament testimony rather than the direct working of the Spirit. And it was this evangelism, in turn, which strained the relations between Campbell's "reformers" and Baptists to the breaking point. Walter Scott later made many other contributions to the Restoration Movement. He spent another 30 years preaching, and often preached with an eloquence that few could equal. He edited several journals including the *Evangelist;* and he served in 1836 as the first president of Bacon College in Georgetown, Kentucky, the first brotherhood college. But Scott's unique legacy to the Restoration Movement had been left as Mahoning evangelist – the proclamation of faith in the Messiah and baptism for the remission of sins, Scott believed, was "the gospel restored."

The Separation

The growing tension between Campbell's "reformers" and the Baptists brought the two groups to the breaking point between 1827 and 1830. Actually, the separation was a gradual process and had begun earlier. As early as 1823, it will be recalled, the Redstone Association had planned to excommunicate Campbell but was thwarted by his transfer to the Mahoning Association. Two years later, the Redstone Association refused to seat any church that had not officially accepted the Philadelphia Confession of Faith; and in 1826, the association divided as ten churches withdrew fellowship from 13 others which stood with the "reformers." This was the first instance of an Association's taking action against the "reformers." But it was only the beginning.

In Kentucky, several Baptist associations were divided. At the North District Association meeting in 1827, a church brought formal charges against "one of the preachers" in the association, without naming him. The charges were trivial compared with the real differences between the "reformers" and Baptists and included such things as reading from Campbell's translation of the New Testament. After the charges were read, Raccoon John Smith, one of the most colorful characters in the Restoration Movement, jumped to his feet and said, "I plead guilty to them all." A bitter debate ensued, and the charges were tabled for a year. But within that year the association reported 900 baptisms, most of them by Smith, and the "reformers" gained control of the association. In 1831 the association dissolved itself out of existence, as the Mahoning Association had done a year earlier.

One of the most important events in the process of separation came in 1929, when the Beaver Association in western Pennsylvania adopted an "Anathema" condemning Campbell and the Mahoning Association. The Beaver Anathema was published in many Baptist journals and was used as a pattern by other associations in withdrawing from the "reformers." The "errors" condemned in the Beaver Anathema provide an excellent summary of some of the major differences between the "reformers" and the Baptists:

They, the Reformers, maintain that there is no promise of salvation without baptism.

That baptism should be administered by all who say they believe that Jesus Christ is the Son of God, without examination on any other point.

That there is no direct operation of the Holy Spirit on the mind prior to baptism.

That baptism procures the remission of sins and the gift of the Holy Spirit.

That no creed is necessary for the church but the Scriptures as they stand.

The Campbells' 17 year marriage with the Baptists was a precarious union at best, and when the divorce came, either party might have charged the other with considerable mental cruelty. The union had worked decidedly to the "reformers" advantage, for it had given Campbell an opportunity to sow his views, like tares, among the Baptist wheat. As a result, scores of Baptist preachers, many churches, and even entire associations had accepted Campbell's call for reformation and Walter Scott's evangelism. Ultimately, the Baptists realized that major surgery was required, but by then it was not easy to separate the tares from the wheat. The Baptists sometimes found that entire associations had fallen victim to the tares. When the divorce became final after 1830, instead of a single Brush Run Church with a handful of members, the Campbell reformation had churches scattered over several states with well over 10,000 members, most of them ex-Baptists.

Questions for review and discussion

1. How did the restoration principle finally lead the Campbells to adopt immersion?
2. Did the adoption of immersion bring the Campbells closer to the goal of unity? Or farther away from it?
3. How did Campbell spread his views among the Baptists?
4. How could Alexander Campbell's writings in the *Christian Baptist* be seen as a continuation of the program proposed in the *Declaration and Address?* How were the *Christian Baptist* and *Declaration and Address* similar? How were they different?
5. Give a sketch of Walter Scott's life. What did he contribute to the Restoration Movement? Why was this contribution so important?
6. What were the differences that resulted in the separation of Campbell's "reformers" from the Baptists?
7. Identify the following:

Bill Humble, PhD.

(1) Matthias Luse
(2) Redstone Association
(3) "Sermon on the Law"
(4) W. L. Maccalla
(5) Christian Baptist
(6) George Forrester
(7) "The gospel restored"
(8) Mahoning Association
(9) Philadelphia Confession of Faith
(10) Raccoon John Smith
(11) Beaver Anathema

Chapter 6
The Movements Converge

The separation of Campbell's "reformers" from the Baptists prepared the way for the next important event in restoration history – the uniting of the Stone and Campbell movements. As long as the "reformers" were a reforming party within the Baptist denomination, any thought of merging with Stone's Christians would have been premature. Still, as the two restoration groups spread through the same areas, contacts between them were inevitable. The Stone movement was strong in Kentucky, and Campbell first visited the state in 1823 for his debate with Maccalla. He was received so cordially by Kentucky Baptists that he made a three month tour of the state the following year. He visited Georgetown, met Barton W. Stone for the first time, and saw the similarity in their pleas for New Testament Christianity. The *Christian Baptist* soon had a large circulation in Kentucky, and this led many Baptists to adopt views which Stone had long been preaching in their state.

In Ohio, too, the movements were spreading through the same areas. When the Mahoning Association selected Walter Scott as evangelist, three Christian preachers were visitors at the meeting. Later, seeing the success of Scott's "faith, repentance and baptism for the remission of sins" evangelism, they began preaching the same message. According to Scott, one of them, Joseph Gaston "was the very first Christian minister who received the gospel after its restoration." Soon, Gaston and Scott were traveling and preaching together through the Western Reserve of Ohio.

Similarities

As contacts between the two movements became frequent, the similarities in their basic beliefs were obvious.

(1) Both accepted the Scripture as the sole authority for Christian faith and denied that creedal statements should be bound on the church.

(2) Both pleaded for Christian unity on the basis of a return to the Bible. Writing in 1831, Stone commented, "For nearly 30 years we have taught that sectarianism was antichristian, and that all Christians should be united in the one body of Christ – the same they teach."

(3) Both had reacted against the Calvinist theology of Presbyterianism and denied such doctrines as predestination and the limited atonement. Instead, they believed that the gospel should be preached to all men and that anyone could believe and obey it.

(4) Both rejected infant sprinkling, and practiced the immersion of believers. And both taught that there was some relation between baptism and the forgiveness of sins.

(5) Both refused to wear unscriptural or sectarian names.

(6) Both regarded denominational organizations such as presbyteries, synods and associations as unscriptural.

And differences

But there were also differences in faith between the two groups. And even through the similarities far outweighed the differences, their disagreements were serious enough to cause concern.

(1) They disagreed about names. The Campbell movement, though often called "reformers," preferred to be called Disciples, while the Stone movement insisted on wearing only the name Christian. Writing in 1831, Stone stated that one reason why the groups were not united was "that we have taken different names" and he went on to insist that the name Christian was "given by divine authority, and designed to supersede all other names of the Lord's followers." After the two groups united, both names continued to be used. When a hymn book was published in 1835, it was first called *The Disciples' Hymn Book*, but Stone protested and in later printings the name was changed to *The Christian Hymn Book.*

(2) The two movements also differed in the emphasis which they placed on immersion. Even though Stone's Christians practiced immersion, they did not insist that it was essential to the remission of sins, as Campbell's Disciples did. Writing about this difference, Stone stated that the doctrine of baptism for the remission of sins "had not generally obtained amongst us, though some few had received it and practiced accordingly." As a result of their divergent views about baptism, Campbell and Stone disagreed about whether it was proper to commune with the unimmersed. Stone was willing to fellowship the unimmersed, but Campbell was not.

(3) Another difference involved the Lord's Supper. As Stone said, "They insisted also upon weekly communion, which we had neglected."

(4) Finally, the two groups were both evangelistic in spirit, but their evangelistic methods were quite different. The Stone movement had originated in the second great awakening, and its preachers stressed the emotional side of religion and encouraged sinners to "weep and mourn" as they sought salvation. Stone emphasized the role of the Holy Spirit in conversion and feared that the Disciples "were not sufficiently explicit on the influence of the Spirit." Campbell and Scott, on the other hand, emphasized the role of reason in conversion. Faith was seen as an act of the reason more than the emotion, and was defined as an acceptance of the New Testament message that Jesus was the Messiah.

Unity achieved

The similarities between the Disciples and Christians far outweighed the differences, and after 1830 leaders of both groups began to consider the possibility of unity. Stone wrote in 1831, "The question is going the round of society, and is often proposed to us, Why are not you and the Reformed Baptists one people? or, Why are you not united? We have uniformly answered, In spirit we are united." Campbell replied, "I think the question of union and cooperation is one which deserves the attention of all them who believe the ancient gospel and desire to see the ancient order of things restored." But since both movements stressed the autonomy of each local church, unity would have to come gradually. The only way it could be realized would be for congregations of the two groups to extend fellowship to one another or merge. The first such merger occurred at Millersburg, Kentucky, on April 24, 1831. There

Story of the Restoration

was a church representing each movement in Millersburg, and they agreed that they were "one as far as faith and practice was concerned" and simply began meeting together as one congregation.

John T. Johnson, a Kentucky preacher associated with the Campbell movement, probably did more to bring the Disciples and Christians together than any other leader of either group. Johnson (1788-1856) was a lawyer who had served two terms in the United States Congress. He had a brother, Richard M. Johnson, who remained in politics and became Vice President of the United States. But John T. Johnson was converted to the restoration plea and renounced politics for the pulpit. Alexander Campbell commended his decision, "Sir, in *descending* from the forum and legislative hall to proclaim the crucified Savior, you have *ascended* far above all earthly crowns."

Johnson and Barton W. Stone both lived in Georgetown, Kentucky, and were warm friends. In November 1831, Stone preached in a meeting at Johnson's Great Crossing church, and the two men discussed the possibilities of unity. Two other leaders, Raccoon John Smith and John Rogers, joined the discussions, and the four men agreed to call a general meeting and see if the members of the two fellowships desired unity. Two meetings were held. The first was at Georgetown, December 23-26, 1831 and the second at Lexington over New Year's weekend, 1832. Raccoon John Smith was the spokesman for the Disciples at the Lexington meeting and, after pleading for unity, he concluded, "Let us, then, my brethren, be no longer Campbellites or Stoneites, New Lights or Old Lights, or any other kind of lights, but let us come to the Bible and to the Bible alone, as the only book in the world that can give us all the light we need." On this basis he and Stone exchanged the right hand of fellowship – an action symbolizing the uniting of the two groups.

Several steps were taken to encourage unity among the scattered churches. Raccoon John Smith (Disciple) and John Rogers (Christian) traveled together through Kentucky, urging the brethren to unite in every community where there were two congregations. And Barton Stone invited John T. Johnson to become associate editor of the *Christian Messenger*, a journal which Stone had founded in 1826. Johnson asked in the *Messenger*, "What could we do but unite? We both compared notes. We found ourselves congregated on the same divine creed, the Bible. We had the same King – the same faith – the same law ... We could not do otherwise than unite in Christian love." The brethren of both restoration movements evidently shared Johnson's spirit, for within a few years the two movements had become one brotherhood.

Barton Stone sensed the significance of what happened at Lexington, and afterward he declared, "This union ... I view as the noblest act of my life." And what was the significance of the merger? Perhaps above all else, the uniting of the two groups demonstrated the validity of their goals and methods. Thomas Campbell's *Declaration and Address,* it will be remembered, had emphasized two ideas: the unity of all Christians, and the restoration of New Testament Christianity as the means of attaining this unity. And what Thomas Campbell had envisioned had actually been achieved when the Christians and Disciples merged into one brotherhood. Independently, the two movements had resolved to discard all creedal loyalties, be guided by New Testament authority, and restore the faith and practices of the first century church; and the results of these independent efforts were so strikingly similar that they compelled unity. Thus, what happened at Lexington in 1832 was a demonstration – in actual practice – that the restoration principle could produce unity.

Unfortunately, this has not always been true. The quest for the New Testament pattern has sometimes led to controversy, as Christians have disagreed about instrumental music, missionary societies, orphan homes and other questions. And all too often these disagreements have resulted in divisions within the restoration movement. But it is not true, as some have charged, that the restoration principle is always divisive. The one united brotherhood which resulted from the Lexington unity meeting in 1832 was proof that the restoration quest could produce unity.

A decade of growth

The decade following the uniting of the Stone and Campbell forces was a period of consolidation and growth for the Restoration Movement. The many religious journals published through the brotherhood contributed to this growth. Since an "official" brotherhood journal was impossible, any preacher was free to become an editor, and many did. At least 28 journals were published during the 1830's, some short-lived, but others had thousands of subscribers and were more permanent. Alexander Campbell's *Millennial Harbinger* led the field. The *Harbinger* had superseded the *Christian Baptist* in 1830, as Campbell had come to believe that a more constructive spirit was needed instead of the earlier iconoclasm. The name *Millennial Harbinger* reflected Campbell's optimistic faith that a golden age for Christianity was dawning. Barton W. Stone had begun his *Christian Messenger* in 1826 announcing as his guiding principle, "Let the unity of Christians be our polar star." Stone continued the *Christian Messenger* until his death in 1844. Another important journal was Walter Scott's *Evangelist,* begun in 1832 and continued for more than a decade.

The growth of the Restoration Movement was also reflected in the establishment of its first colleges. The first was Bacon College, which was begun at Georgetown, Kentucky, in 1836 with Walter Scott serving as its first president. Bethany College was founded by Alexander Campbell in 1840, and according to Campbell it was "not a theological school" but was the only "literary and scientific" college in the world "founded upon the Bible as the basis of all true science and true learning." One importance of Bethany College lies in the future restoration leaders that it trained: J. W. McGarvey, Moses Lard, and a host of others. The third of the Christian colleges was Franklin College, founded by Tolbert Fanning near Nashville, Tennessee in 1845. Franklin College continued only until the Civil War, but during these years it trained many preachers who would be prominent in the South after the Civil War.

Debates were another important means of disseminating the restoration plea. Alexander Campbell's first debates with Walker and Maccalla were typical of the religious controversy of the time and aroused only local interest, but in 1829 Campbell defended the Christian faith in a debate which brought him national prominence. His opponent was Robert Owen, internationally known social reformer and atheist, who had founded a utopian social community at New Harmony, Indiana. The debate was held in Cincinnati, Ohio, and involved the evidences for Christianity against Owen's charge that all religions had hindered the progress of civilization. Eight years later in 1837, Cincinnati was the scene of another debate that attracted national attention, Campbell became the champion of Protestantism against the Catholic bishop of Cincinnati, John B. Purcell. The issues in this unique debate included the claim that the Catholic church is "catholic, apostolic and holy," such doctrines as purgatory and transubstantiation, and the charge that Catholicism was anti-American. The debates with Owen and Purcell gave Campbell a national prestige which he had not enjoyed earlier, and they set a pattern of "contending for the faith" which encouraged a controversial spirit in the movement. Following Campbell's example, later generations of Christian preachers have engaged in thousands of debates with opponents of many denominations. It is only in the mid twentieth century that such debates have begun to decline in popularity.

The story of the Restoration Movement in the decades between the Lexington unity meeting and the Civil War is one of remarkable optimism, vitality and numerical growth. The geographic center of the movement was the Ohio Valley – Bethany, Lexington, Cincinnati and westward – but radiating from this center it spread rapidly in every direction, into the South, through Indiana and Illinois, west of the Mississippi into Missouri and Iowa. The united movement probably had between 20,000 and 25,000 members in 1832, but 30 years later the estimated membership was nearly 200,000. The geographic spread of the Restoration

Movement had been so rapid that by 1860 there were 17 states where at least a thousand Christians could be counted. According to Garrison and DeGroot's estimate, they were:

Kentucky – 45,000
Indiana – 25,000
Ohio – 25,000
Missouri – 20,000
Illinois – 15,000
Tennessee – 12,285
Iowa – 10,000
Virginia – 8,430
New York – 2,500
North Carolina – 2,500
Texas – 2,500
Alabama – 2,458
Mississippi – 2,450
Arkansas – 2,257
California – 1,223
Georgia – 1,100
Michigan – 1,000

Questions for review and discussion

1. How were the Stone and Campbell movements similar?
2. What were the main differences between them?
3. Describe the events that led to the uniting of the two movements.
4. How did the uniting of the Stone and Campbell movements show the validity of the *Declaration and Address*?

Story of the Restoration

5. What factors contributed to the growth of the movement through the 1830's and 1840's?
6. What was the significance of Campbell's debates with Owen and Purcell?
7. In what states was the restoration Movement strongest by 1860?
8. Identify the following:
   (1) John Gaston
   (2) Millersburg, KY
   (3) John T. Johnson
   (4) Christian Messenger
   (5) Millennial Harbinger
   (6) Bethany College
   (7) Franklin College
   (8) Raccoon John Smith
   (9) John Rogers

Chapter 7
The Missionary Society Controversy

The 1830s were a time of unity, optimism, and remarkable growth for the Restoration Movement, but they were also a time when seeds of later controversy were being sown – serious controversy which would ultimately rupture the unity of the movement. The 1830's saw the appearance of "cooperation meetings" among the churches. The next decade saw the organization of the American Christian Missionary Society (1849), and this development, in turn, led to controversy which continued until the movement had been divided.

The cooperation meeting

In 1831-1832 Alexander Campbell published a series of seven articles on "The Cooperation of Churches" in the *Millennial Harbinger*. Campbell believed that the world could never be evangelized unless the churches cooperated in the proclamation of the gospel, and his articles were a plea for this cooperation. Campbell argued that the New Testament provided examples of churches' cooperating with one another (2 Cor. 8, etc.) and this provided scriptural authority for church cooperation. But he insisted that the exact details of how churches should cooperate were left to the discretion of every generation. Campbell suggested, as one example of how congregations might work together, that all the churches in his home county might have an annual general meeting at which plans would be made for evangelizing the area, an evangelist selected, and provisions made for his support.

Following Campbell's suggestions, churches in many areas began to organize "cooperation meetings" through the decade of the 1830's. For example, a meeting was held at Wellsburg, Virginia, near Campbell's home on April 12, 1834 to organize such a meeting. The 13 churches represented agreed to employ two evangelists, appointed a treasurer to receive funds from the churches for their support, and set up a committee of 13 to supervise the evangelists and their work. However, there was opposition to this "Wellsburg Cooperation" and a year later it was dissolved. Instead, the churches decided that a cooperation meeting should be limited to the number of congregations necessary to sustain a single evangelist.

The churches moved slowly in the organization of such cooperation meetings through the decade of the 1830's, but after 1840 the movement gained momentum. State-wide cooperation meetings began to be held. Illinois Christians held a state-wide meeting at Springfield in 1834, attended by Barton W. Stone. The 1840 *Millennial Harbinger* carried announcements of cooperation meetings in six states: Illinois, Virginia, Missouri, Ohio, Kentucky and Indiana – an indication that the meetings were gaining brotherhood approval.

"The burnt child dreads the fire"

There were some preachers who viewed the cooperation meetings with misgivings. No sooner had Campbell begun his first articles calling for cooperation than one brother objected that such a "combination" of churches was wrong. T. M. Henley, a prominent Virginian, wrote Campbell in 1836 that it seemed to him "like a departure from the simplicity of the Christian institution to have cooperation meetings with *Presidents and Secretaries,* calling for the *Messengers* of the churches, and laying off districts." Henley recalled that this was how Baptist associations had originated in Virginia, and remembering how the Christians had been treated by Virginia Baptist associations, he commented, "The burnt child dreads the fire."

After warning against cooperation meetings, Henley insisted that he also favored cooperation and proposed an alternative – cooperation through a local church. He recommended that if a congregation wished to send out an evangelist but was unable to support him, it could invite other churches to assist. The elders of one congregation would oversee the work, receive funds from other churches, and report their use to the contributing churches.

There are many early examples of churches following this plan of cooperating through one church. For example, three Kentucky churches raised a fund of several hundred dollars for preaching the gospel in 1842. One of the churches, Georgetown, was entrusted with the funds, and the Georgetown elders employed John T. Johnson to work under their oversight. When other churches adopted this plan, Johnson commended them for following "the same scriptural principles" of cooperation.

Campbell's call for organization

If there were some who questioned the cooperation meetings, there were others, including Alexander Campbell, who believed the cooperation meetings had not gone far enough. Campbell began a series of articles entitled "The Nature of the Christian Organization" in 1841, and when the 16 article series was concluded two years later, Campbell had proposed the establishment of a "general organization" among the churches. The church, Campbell argued, is described as "the body of Christ," and a body must necessarily be organized. Admitting that the New Testament does not provide for any general organization of the church, Campbell concluded the creation of such an organization is left to the judgment of the churches. He proposed that the churches hold a convention and devise a general organization. Such an organization, according to Campbell, would leave the churches free to manage their own internal affairs, but it would enable them to concentrate their resources in preaching the gospel, and it would have authority to ordain evangelists and settle disputes within a local church.

Campbell's old friend Walter Scott was strongly opposed to Campbell's proposal for a general organization. Campbell had stated repeatedly that the churches were "deficient in organization," but Scott did not agree. He insisted that when a church had elders and deacons, it was "already organized," and he claimed that this was the view of the entire brotherhood. And he asked, rather sharply, "Who made brother Campbell an organizer over us?"

The first brotherhood organization was the American Christian Bible Society which was organized in Cincinnati, Ohio, early in 1845. D. S. Burnet, a prominent Cincinnati preacher – rather than Alexander Campbell – took the lead in organizing the Bible society. The purpose of the society was "to aid in the distribution of the Sacred Scriptures" throughout the world. The constitution, which was drawn up by Burnet, provided for officers, an annual meeting, and the organization of auxiliary societies which would place their surplus funds at the disposal of the Cincinnati society. D. S. Burnet was elected president of the new Bible society and hailed it as a "holy cause" which should "enlist all our affections."

The Bible society received enthusiastic support from most of the brotherhood periodicals, but Campbell announced in the *Millennial Harbinger* that he opposed it. Campbell's attitude is somewhat surprising, in view of his frequent articles calling for a "general organization" among the churches. The reason which he gave for opposing the society was the fact that it had been organized by a few Cincinnati brethren rather than a general convention of the churches. But there may have been more to Campbell's opposition than this. Arthur Crihfield later charged bluntly that if the Bible society "had commenced at Bethany," Campbell would not have opposed it; and he may have been right. Campbell's attitude resulted in a sharp editorial controversy between him and the Bible society's supporters. Campbell and D. S. Burnet were close friends and were able to reconcile their differences, but Campbell did not relent in his hostility to the society.

American Christian Missionary Society

Early in 1849, Campbell resumed his efforts to persuade the brotherhood of the need for "a more efficient organization" of the churches. Since the autonomy of each local church had been a cherished principle in the Restoration Movement, there were obviously serious problems in the proposal. How could independent churches hold a convention to consider an organization? Who could call such a convention? Where would it be held? And would the brotherhood accept an organization? The brotherhood periodicals discussed these questions through 1849, and an editorial consensus gradually emerged – a general convention would be held at Cincinnati on October 23, 1849, in conjunction with the annual meeting of the Bible society.

When the Cincinnati convention convened, ten states were represented by the 156 people present. Many prominent brotherhood preachers were there, but not Campbell. Whatever the reason for his absence, Campbell's views were represented by son-in-law W. K. Pendleton and his shadow fell over the sessions. It was generally understood that one action of the convention would be the organization of a missionary society for the brotherhood. But it was not clear how such a society would be related to the Bible society. One suggestion was that the Bible society be reorganized to include a "missionary department," but such a plan would probably not have won Campbell's approval. Pendleton, on the other hand, proposed that an independent missionary society be organized and commended to the brotherhood as the "chief object of importance" in their benevolent work. But this course would have offended the many brethren who had been supporting the Bible society.

This problem was the most difficult one which the convention faced, and it was solved in the good American tradition of compromise. The convention decided: (1) that a missionary society would be organized, (2) that the Bible society would be commended to the brotherhood for its support, and (3) that the two societies would be instructed to work together.

D. S. Burnet presided over the Cincinnati convention and helped draft the constitution for the American Christian Missionary Society. It is not surprising, then, that the constitution for the new missionary society was patterned after that of the Bible society. The constitution provided that the object of the missionary society would be "to promote the preaching of the gospel in destitute places" throughout the world. The society would consist of Annual Delegates, Life Members, and Life Directors. Anyone could become a Life Member by contributing $20 to the society or a Life Director by contributing $100. Any church could appoint a "delegate" to the society's annual convention by contributing $20 to the society. The constitution also provided for officers (president, 20 vice presidents, two secretaries, treasurer, managers), an annual meeting of the entire society, and an Executive Board to transact business between meetings.

The final action of the convention was to authorize a letter to Alexander Campbell expressing sorrow that he had been unable to attend the meeting and informing Campbell that he had been elected president of the new missionary society. Shortly afterward, Campbell wrote that his expectations from the convention had been "more than realized" (even though the missionary society was hardly the "general organization" Campbell had advocated). And he withdrew his objections to the Bible society since it had now been endorsed by a brotherhood convention. Campbell also accepted the presidency of the missionary society and served in the office for the rest of his life (1849-1866).

The first work which the society undertook was to send Dr. James T. Barclay and his family of Scottsville, Virginia, to Jerusalem. There was "magic in the name of Jerusalem," as Walter Scott put it, and the brotherhood responded eagerly to the idea of planting the church in the city where it had begun. The Barclay family arrived in Jerusalem in 1850, but the work was very discouraging and was discontinued in 1853 as the Crimean War loomed over the Middle East. Other early activities of the missionary society included sending Alexander Cross, a freed slave, to Liberia, Africa, and J. O. Beardslee to Jamaica.

A decade of opposition

The American Christian Missionary Society never had the support of the entire brotherhood. There was opposition immediately after its establishment and it was never silenced. After the Civil War the opposition became so widespread that ultimately the church was divided, though it should be understood that the missionary society was not the only issue in the final division.

Jacob Creath, Jr. was the most outspoken early critic of the society. When Campbell had begun publication of the *Christian Baptist* in 1823, he had denounced missionary societies. The churches of the New Testament age, Campbell wrote, "were not fractured into missionary societies," for the early Christians "knew nothing of the *hobbies* of modern times." They dared not "transfer to a missionary society, or Bible society, or education society, *a cent or a prayer,* lest in so doing they should rob the church of its glory, and exalt the inventions of men above the wisdom of God. *In their church capacity alone they moved.*" Quite obviously, Campbell had changed his views in the quarter century between 1823 and the founding of the American Christian Missionary Society. Creath reminded Campbell of these earlier views, and he wrote, "If you were right in the *Christian Baptist,* you are wrong now. If you are right now, you were wrong then." And Creath charged that supporters of the society had "totally abandoned" the rule that "the Bible alone is the religion of Protestants."

There were also churches, and even groups of churches, which adopted resolutions opposing the missionary society. The best known of these, adopted by the church in Connelsville, Pennsylvania, stated that the church was "not *a* missionary society, but emphatically and pre-eminently *the* missionary society – the only one authorized by Jesus Christ." And if the church was the divine missionary society, "all other societies for this purpose are not only unscriptural, but they are unnecessary and uncalled for." The Connelsville church also objected to the provision that membership in the society was based on money; and they charged that the society was "a dangerous precedent – a departure from the principles" of the Restoration Movement. Virginia Christians held a general meeting at Emmaus in May, 1850, and adopted resolutions stating they could not work through the missionary society. Since Dr. Barclay was a Virginian, they wanted to support his work and planned an "independent State effort" to raise funds for the Jerusalem mission.

The most important opponent of the missionary society in the pre-Civil War years was Tolbert Fanning. Fanning (1810-1874), who spent most of his adult life around Nashville, Tennessee, was the most influential Christian preacher in the South during the 1850's and 1860's. Fanning was a talented man of diverse interests. He helped found the Tennessee Agricultural Society and edited its journal, the *Agriculturalist*. He founded Franklin College, trained many preachers, and edited several religious journals. When the American Christian Missionary Society was founded, Fanning was elected a vice president (though not present at the Cincinnati convention), and he supported the society through the early 1850's. But gradually, Fanning came to question the missionary society. He founded the *Gospel Advocate* in 1855 and stated that his "chief purpose " in establishing the new journal was to examine the subjects of church organization and Christian cooperation. The spirit of Fanning's early articles in the *Gospel Advocate* was strikingly similar to that of Alexander Campbell in the early *Christian Baptist*. Fanning wrote, "The Church of God is the only divinely authorized Missionary, Bible, Sunday School and Temperance Society; the only institution in which the Heavenly Father will be honored ... and through no other agency can man glorify his Maker." It was wrong for Christians to "do the work of the church through merely human agencies."

Fanning realized that foreign missions would require the support of many churches, but he urged that it should be done through "the agreement and cooperation of the churches" rather than through the society. Using the Barclay mission to Jerusalem as an example, Fanning stated that it would have been better if Dr. Barclay had been commissioned by his home congregation and if that church had asked the financial help of sister churches. Had this been done, Fanning argued, the Barclay mission would have had "the authority of Scriptural examples" in its favor.

During the years just before the Civil War a majority of Southern Christians came to share Fanning's view that there was no Biblical authority for missionary societies. Yet there was no sense of alienation from those who supported the society. In 1859 Fanning attended the society's annual convention in Cincinnati and was invited to address the convention and describe the mission work that Tennessee churches were doing. Fanning took advantage of the occasion to state that many Southern Christians could not conscientiously support the society. Next, he described how three Tennessee congregations were cooperating "as churches, without the aid of a Missionary Society" to support J. J. Trott in mission work among the Cherokee Indians. After these jabs at the society, Fanning must have reassured the assembly when he said, "But I am happy to say, that from what I have heard on this floor, we are one people. With us all there is one faith, one God, one body and one spirit."

Thus, as the nation reached a critical juncture in its history and the Civil War loomed ahead, the Restoration Movement had also reached a crossroad. The Christians in North and South held opposing views on an important doctrinal issue – whether the missionary society was scriptural – but as yet, these differences had produced no sense of division.

Questions for review and discussion

1. Describe the early cooperation meetings.

Story of the Restoration

2. Why were some opposed to the cooperation meetings? Explain: "The burnt child dreads the fire."
3. How did Campbell argue for a "general organization" of the churches? Do you agree – or disagree – with him?
4. What was the American Christian Bible Society? Did Campbell support this society?
5. Describe the events leading to the organization of the missionary society. Where were its first missionaries sent?
6. Did Campbell support the missionary society? Had he always favored such organizations?
7. Describe the early opposition to the society. What reasons were given for opposing it?
8. Identify the following:
    (1) Wellsburg cooperation meeting
    (2) T. M. Henley
    (3) D. S. Burnet
    (4) James T. Barclay
    (5) Jacob Creath, Jr.
    (6) Connelsville resolutions
    (7) Tolbert Fanning
    (8) Gospel Advocate
    (9) J. J. Trott

Chapter 8
The Civil War Ordeal

The outbreak of the Civil War was an agonizing test of whether the United States could endure as one nation. It was also a test of whether the Restoration Movement could endure as one people. The sectional struggle placed an unusually heavy strain on the Christians' unity, for in 1860 they had about 1,200 churches in the North and about 800 in the South. Furthermore, many of these churches were clustered in the Ohio Valley and in such border states as Kentucky and Missouri, areas where loyalties were so divided that Christian was often set against Christian, brother against brother, father against son.

The tension that was felt in countless border state congregations is illustrated in a letter that Thomas Munnell of Mount Sterling, Kentucky, wrote to David Oliphant in 1862. According to Munnell, in many Kentucky churches Union and Confederate sympathizers were attempting to worship together, sing the same songs, eat and drink the same bread and wine, and say "Amen" to the same prayers. The atmosphere was so tense that if preachers had supported either side from the pulpit, they would have destroyed half the churches in Kentucky in a month. Munnell wrote, "We hope not to divide into North and South churches as other large religious bodies have." And he pleaded, "Brother should not go to war with brother."

Christian pacifism

The plea that "brother should not go to war with brother" was often heard among the Christians, and this was a spiritual strength which helped to compensate for their geographic weakness. Except for Walter Scott, all the early restoration leaders had been pacifists. When the Civil War began, a majority of the preachers and editors – Alexander Campbell, Benjamin Franklin, J. W. McGarvey, Moses E. Lard, Robert Milligan, Tolbert Fanning, David Lipscomb and a host of others – counseled non-participation. J. W. McGarvey declared that he would do everything he could to keep his brethren from enlisting for military service. He wrote, "I would rather, ten thousand times, be killed for refusing to fight than to fall in battle, or come home victorious with the blood of my brethren on my hands." McGarvey asked his brethren what the twelve apostles would have done had they been living during the Civil War, six in the North and six in the South. Would they have urged Christians to enlist? McGarvey described himself as "standing in between my brethren and the battlefield, with the New Testament in hand, warning them, as they hope for heaven, to keep the peace." Robert Milligan was another pacifist. He had become president of Transylvania College in Kentucky in 1859 and managed to keep the school open throughout the war – the only college in Kentucky to do this.

Shortly after the war began, J. W. McGarvey and 13 other prominent Missouri preachers signed a plea calling upon Christians not to participate in the fighting. This plea was published in many brotherhood journals. The preachers warned that any who engaged in the "fratricidal strife" would incur God's displeasure; and they pleaded that the church should remain a united body. Similarly, the elders and evangelists of several Tennessee churches met at Beech Grove, Tennessee, in 1862 and drafted a letter to Jefferson Davis, President of the Confederacy, requesting that Christians be exempt from military service. They declared that the South's draft law would bring "indescribable distress" to Christians who objected to military service. As a result, the Confederate government granted conscientious objector's status to the Christians, and after the was was over, David Lipscomb claimed that Tennessee Christians had been "almost a unit" in refusing military service.

On the other hand, there were thousands of Christians on both sides of the Mason-Dixon line who enlisted in the armies. Alexander Campbell's son wore the Confederate gray, as did Barton W. Stone, Jr. Moreover, there were some preachers who supported the war effort in each section. James A. Garfield became a Colonel in the Union army, made recruiting speeches on the steps of churches, and persuaded many of his former students at Hiram College to join his regiment. Garfield fought from Shiloh to Chickamauga, was elected to Congress, and finally became President of the United States. And in the South T. B. Larimore, B. F. Hall, Addison and Randolph Clark, Austin McGary and General R. M. Gano wore the Confederate gray.

There were two men – Benjamin Franklin and Tolbert Fanning – who illustrated the tension which many Christians felt between the demands of God and Caesar. Each man was the most popular preacher in the brotherhood in his section throughout the 1860's, Franklin in the North and Fanning in the South. Each was a pacifist; but when the Civil War came, each man felt strong sectional loyalties.

When Franklin was criticized for not allowing political issues to be discussed in his influential journal, the *American Christian Review*, he protested that he had not "one spark of disloyal feeling toward the Union" but loved it "next to the government of God." Tolbert Fanning, on the other hand, believed just as strongly in the right of the Southern cause. He believed the war had been caused by "infidel preachers" – he named men like Theodore Parker, Ralph Waldo Emerson and Henry Ward Beecher – who "trampled underfoot the word of God and the constitution." Was the South justified in resisting the Union? Fanning replied, "If people were ever justified in resisting encroachments, we conscientiously believe the citizens of the Confederate States are." But he hastened to add, "All this we have spoken as a citizen of the world, and not as a member of the family of God."

Notwithstanding their strong sectional loyalties, Franklin and Fanning both believed that the Christian had a higher obligation, and this demanded that he stand aloof from the Civil War. Franklin wrote, "We will not take up arms against, fight or kill the brethren we have labored for twenty years to bring into the Kingdom of God." Similarly, Fanning counseled Christians to avoid military service. He wrote in July, 1861, "Both parties claim the sanction of Heaven, and very earnestly call upon God for help. Both cannot be right." And he added, "It may be that God intends to prove his people, and ... the war may be the occasion for the test." Four years later, a man of the North also noted sadly that North and South both prayed to the same God and read the same Bible. He, like Fanning, saw the war as God's judgment on both North and South, but he said humbly, "The judgments of the Lord are true and righteous altogether" – this was Abraham Lincoln.

On record for the Union

The first wartime meeting of the American Christian Missionary Society was held at Cincinnati in October, 1861. The South was not represented. The crucial question facing the convention was whether the society would restrict itself to missionary concerns or would take a stand favoring the North in the Civil War. The issue was raised by Dr. John P. Robison of Bedford, Ohio, who introduced a resolution calling on "brethren everywhere to do all in their power to sustain the proper and constitutional authorities of the Union." James A. Garfield, appearing before the convention in the uniform of a Union officer, made a short speech favoring the resolution and it was adopted with only one dissenting vote. However, the missionary society had to adjourn for a ten-minute "recess" before the vote was taken, so technically the motion was accepted by a "mass meeting" of those present – not by the missionary society in formal session.

When news of the missionary society's action reached Southern Christians, Tolbert Fanning, who had been pleading with Southern brethren to remain aloof from the hostilities, was heartbroken and angered. Just before the *Gospel Advocate* was forced to suspend publication for the duration of the war, Fanning informed his readers that the missionary society had adopted resolutions approving "the wholesale murder" of the Southern people. As Fanning saw it, the missionary society was encouraging "thousands of professed servants of the Prince of Peace" to enlist in the Union armies.

Fanning's reaction was blunt and angry, sad and ominous. If he should ever again see the preachers who had passed the pro-Union resolution, Fanning asked, "Can we fraternize with them as brethren? He saw his own course clearly. Unless there was thorough repentance on their part, Fanning did not see how he could "ever regard preachers who enforce political opinions by the sword, in any other light than monsters in intention, if not in very deed"; and he pleaded, "How can Christian men of the South do otherwise?" Strong language, indeed, from the one who addressed the missionary society's convention only two years earlier and had said, "We are one people."

A second loyalty resolution

Two years later, in 1863, the missionary society adopted an even stronger resolution supporting the North. One reason for the new resolution was increasing pressure on the society from a small but vocal group of militant abolitionists within the brotherhood. Throughout the 1850s the abolitionists – Pardee Butler, Ovid Butler, John Boggs and others – demanded that slavery be denounced as a sin and that Southern slave owners be disfellowshipped. These demands kept the brotherhood in a turmoil. Even Alexander Campbell came in for criticism. Campbell had long opposed slavery, but he saw abolitionism an an even greater danger to the unity of the church. The abolitionists, in turn, denounced Campbell as "soft" on the slavery issue and established a rival college in Indianapolis, Northwestern Christian University, later renamed Butler.

Bill Humble, PhD.

The *Northwestern Christian Magazine*, edited by John Boggs, was established in 1854 to champion the abolitionist cause. The American Christian Missionary Society was denounced for being "implicated in the sin of slavery." The basis of this charge was the fact that Dr. James Barclay had been a slaveholder before becoming the society's first missionary. The abolitionists' hostility to the missionary society became so intense that in 1858 they held a convention in Indianapolis and organized a rival Christian Missionary Society. Organizationally, it was almost identical to the Cincinnati society, but its membership requirements included "No complicity in the crime of American slavery." Thus, even before the outbreak of the Civil War the brotherhood in the North found itself divided with two rival missionary organizations competing for its support. Nor was the abolitionist society disbanded when the war began. John Boggs warned the American Christian Missionary Society that unless it would bear "testimony against slavery as the cause of the present rebellion," the brotherhood would remain divided.

Beset by extreme abolitionist criticism, the American Christian Missionary Society also faced ugly rumors circulating through the North and charging the society with disloyalty to the Union. Thus, when the society met in 1863, it adopted a new loyalty resolution which denounced these rumors as "false and slanderous" and declared its unqualified support of the North.

The society's action alienated many of its former supporters. J. W. McGarvey wrote that the society had destroyed its usefulness and should "cease to exist." Moses E. Lard called the society's resolution a shameful action and warned that if the society ever passed another political resolution, "it should die." Benjamin Franklin, editor of the influential *American Christian Review*, believed the society had abandoned "its legitimate work" in adopting the resolution. And after the war was over, Franklin became the society's most vigorous opponent in the North.

Sectional bitterness

The divisive effect of the missionary society's pro-Union resolutions was soon evident after the war ended. Early in 1866 Tolbert Fanning proposed a "general consultation meeting" of Southern Christians. The Christians in the South, like all Southerners, had suffered great hardships during the war. Communications had been disrupted, religious periodicals had been forced to suspend publication, and preachers had been unable to travel among the churches. Fanning believed that Southern Christians needed to "counsel together" and assess the condition of the church, and he proposed the general meeting for that purpose. The meeting was held at Murfreesboro, Tennessee, in June 1866, and six Southern states were represented.

When Benjamin Franklin read of the proposed meeting, he objected that Northern Christians were excluded and commented, "There is no South or North in our gospel." Fanning's response illustrates the mood of the church in the South. He told Franklin that he doubted "the propriety of a hasty religious *reconstruction*" with Northern brethren. Since they had been "employing the fist of wickedness" against their brethren in the South, Fanning added, "It seems to me that men engaged in such service, may not be very well prepared to engage in genuine spiritual cooperation."

When the *Gospel Advocate* resumed publication in 1866, David Lipscomb lost no time in writing about the wartime resolutions of the missionary society, and his language was more bitter than Fanning's. Lipscomb recalled that he expected the Cincinnati society to strengthen those who were pleading with Christians not to enlist in the armies. But instead, he wrote, "We found only vindictive, murderous spirit ruling its counsels, and encouraging the *Christian (?)* work of *Christians* North robbing and slaughtering Christians South." Lipscomb charged that the society had performed a valuable service for the North in "inducing the followers of the prince of peace to become men of war and blood." Lipscomb recalled that when the war began, nothing had been more effective in restraining Southern Christians from enlisting than Franklin's articles in the *American Christian Review,* for these indicated that Northern Christians were trying to stand aloof from military service and bloodshed. But the missionary society's 1861 resolution had encouraged brethren to enlist in the Union army. The society's resolution, Lipscomb knew, had caused Southern brethren to enlist, and some had not returned. Lipscomb concluded, "We felt, we still feel, that the Society committed a great wrong against the Church and cause of God. We have felt, we still feel, that without evidence of a repentance of the wrong, it should not receive the confidence of the Christian brotherhood."

The missionary society's own records also furnish evidence of the divisive impact of the war. When the society's Board of Managers presented their annual report in 1879, they admitted that the society was fighting a "fearful battle" against its opponents. And the first source of this opposition which they cited was "the alienations produced by the late war."

The Civil War had so shattered the sense of brotherhood between Northern and Southern Christians that they could never again be called "one people" in any meaningful sense. This does not mean that the Civil War was *alone* responsible for the ultimate division. Even before the war the Southerners had accepted a stricter view of the restoration principle, and this had led them to oppose the missionary society. On the other hand, the South's narrower understanding of the restoration principle did not result in division until Civil War bitterness had destroyed the atmosphere of good will in which doctrinal differences between North and South might have been discussed and perhaps resolved. What happened was that two threads of alienation – sectional bitterness and differences in understanding the restoration principle – had become tangled together and had shattered the Christians' oneness. Tolbert Fanning would never again say, as he had told the missionary society in 1859, "We are one people."

Questions for review and discussion

1. What was J. W. McGarvey's attitude toward a Christian's serving in the army during the Civil War? How many preachers agreed with McGarvey?
2. Compare the attitudes of Benjamin Franklin and Tolbert Fanning toward the war.

3. What action did the missionary society take in 1861? Was this action wise?
4. How did abolitionism influence the history of the Restoration Movement?
5. If you had been present for the missionary society's 1863 meeting, would you have voted in favor of their pro-Union resolution?
6. How did David Lipscomb react to the society's wartime resolutions?
7. Historians have often said that the Restoration Movement was not divided by the Civil War. Do you agree?
8. Do you feel that Christians should have refused military service during the Civil War?
9. Identify the following:
   (1) Thomas Munnell
   (2) Beech Grove resolution
   (3) James A. Garfield
   (4) John Boggs
   (5) Christian Missionary Society
   (6) Benjamin Franklin
   (7) Murfreesboro consultation meeting
   (8) Dr. John P. Robison
   (9) Christian pacifism

Chapter 9
The Influence of Editors

It has often been said, "The Restoration Movement has not had *bishops;* it has had *editors.*" And it is true that the editors of brotherhood journals have wielded great influence in shaping the history of the movement. When a church is ruled by bishops (as in the Catholic and Episcopal churches), the power lies in their hands. But when a church believes that each congregation is free from all higher control, there is no office comparable to the Catholic bishop; yet there must be leadership. In the Restoration Movement this leadership has been provided by the editors – editors like Campbell and Stone whose journals charted the course of the movement during its formative years.

The years following the Civil War were fateful ones for the Restoration Movement, and during these years it was the editors, once more, who led the movement. This chapter will describe the roles of five great editors in guiding the church through these crucial years.

Benjamin Franklin and the American Christian Review

The most influential brotherhood journal in the North after the war was the *American Christian Review,* edited by Benjamin Franklin (1812-1878). Franklin had begun preaching in the 1830's, and even though he was a self-made man with little formal education, he became the most popular preacher in the brotherhood during the 1860's and

1870's. He spoke the language of the masses and enjoyed their confidence. He was probably the most popular debater in the church after Campbell, and his many debates contributed to his popularity as a preacher.

Franklin began his career as an editor in 1845. His first journal, *The Reformer* (1845-1847), was followed by the *Western Reformer* (1847-1850) and the Proclamation and Reformer (1850-1853). But Franklin's great influence as an editor was exerted through the *American Christian Review* which he founded in 1856 and continued through the remainder of his life. A monthly during its first two years, the *Review* became a weekly newspaper size journal in 1858 and was soon the most influential paper in the brotherhood. As Franklin described his paper, "The *Review* is intended for and adapted to the masses. It is a plain gospel paper. ... It aims to imitate the style of Jesus and the apostles, and to stand firmly for their teaching in all things." Franklin's *Review* was thoroughly conservative in its approach to New Testament Christianity, strongly opposed to instrumental music and other "innovations" that were coming into the church.

The *Review's* editorial policy toward the American Christian Missionary Society was an important factor in the controversy which rocked the church after the Civil War. Franklin had been a supporter of the society for many years. He had attended the convention which organized the society in 1849. Elected a manager of the society in 1850, he had held some office in the society for 17 consecutive years, including a short term (1856-1857) as corresponding secretary, the most important office in the missionary society. In 1858 he had defended the society in a heated editorial controversy with David Oliphant. But the Civil War turned Franklin's support to opposition. Franklin opposed Christians' serving in the army, and he believed that the missionary society should stay with its "legitimate work" and avoid political pronouncements. When the society adopted its 1863 resolution supporting the Union, Franklin warned that if the society brought "strife and contention" to the church, it should be abandoned. And in 1866 Franklin announced in the *Review* that he could no longer defend the missionary society, but instead had come to believe that it was an unscriptural organization. Franklin's change was a staggering blow to the society and precipitated a decade of controversy among Northern Christians. Nor did the controversy end until the church was divided.

Isaac Errett and the *Christian Standard*

Meanwhile, there was a part of the Northern brotherhood that was becoming increasingly critical of Franklin and the *Review*. These men were more liberal in spirit, and they believed that Franklin was too narrow and dogmatic in his loyalty to the past. What was needed was "a more progressive religion," as they often expressed it. Led by the wealthy Phillips brothers of Pennsylvania, Isaac Errett, James A. Garfield, Dr. J. P. Robison, W. K. Pendleton and others, they determined to launch a new weekly journal, the *Christian Standard,* which would offset the influence of the *Review*. The first issue of the *Standard* appeared on April 7, 1866.

Isaac Errett (1820-1888) was chosen to edit the *Standard,* and it proved to be a very wise choice. Errett had been reared in a Haldanean church of Christ in New York. He learned the printer's trade while yet in his teens, and through it he became interested in writing. Errett, like Franklin, had little formal education, but he had great natural ability, particularly as a writer. He had preached for Ohio churches through the 1840's, and while serving as a minister of the Warren, Ohio, congregation (1851-1856), he attained a reputation beyond local circles. He served as corresponding secretary of the Ohio Missionary Society in 1853 and had some official connection with the Disciples' missionary work through the rest of his life. He held the office of corresponding secretary of the national society for several years, became a co-editor of the *Millennial Harbinger* in 1861, and was closely associated with Alexander Campbell during the last years of Campbell's life.

The *Christian Standard* barely survived its birth. It was well edited and contained such a wide variety of material that it should have appealed to all members of a Christian family. Its founders had assumed that it would have a large circulation, but in this they were mistaken. The paper suffered heavy financial losses, and the stockholders voted to discontinue it but agreed, instead, to transfer ownership to Errett. Eventually, however, the R. W. Carroll Co. of Cincinnati assumed control of the *Standard* and put it on a sound financial basis. Errett continued as editor of the *Standard* from its beginning until his death in 1888 – 22 years later.

The *Standard* was the only weekly journal that supported missionary societies during the years just after the Civil War. The *Review* had taken a stand against the societies in 1866. In the South the *Gospel Advocate* had opposed the society through the late 1850's, and the sectional bitterness which the war had left intensified the opposition. But the missionary society was not the main issue between the *Standard* and the *Gospel Advocate*. The issues which they discussed were whether Christians had a right to engage in military service, who was responsible for the Civil War, and the status of the freedmen in the South. Errett argues that when a government was threatened with rebellion, the sword had a righteous mission to fulfill. He insisted that Christians had been under a "sacred obligation to maintain and defend a government so unrighteously assailed." And he charged that Lipscomb's view that Christians should have nothing to do with government was "a new-born faith" espoused by those "in sympathy with a lost cause."

But the real clash of ideas in the church was in the North, where the *Review* and *Standard* stood opposed on a wide variety of issues. The first serious clash was over the missionary society, and later the issue was instrumental music. But these were only symptomatic of problems that lay deeper. The *Review* was conservative in spirit, more biblical in its approach, and committed to preserving the faith of the past. The *Standard* was more liberal in tone, admitted many new practices as expedients, and was less hostile to departures from traditional ways. Isaac Errett was the first preacher in the movement to accept the title "Reverend" – to the dismay of men like Franklin. Errett advocated a more progressive religion and described his critics as "the loudest croakers against 'progression'." Franklin's views reflected an opposite spirit. "We are heartily sick listening to *progressive* Christians continually talking about a 'higher order of Christianity,' and 'keeping up with the time.' ... These church progressionists progress so rapidly that they frequently transcend the limits of Christian duty." And he warned that they were more interested in "conciliation and compromise" than in converting the world.

David Lipscomb and the *Gospel Advocate*

The most influential journal in the South was the *Gospel Advocate*. Suspended during the war, it resumed publication in 1866 with Tolbert Fanning and David Lipscomb as editors. But Fanning was too busy with other activities to devote much time to the paper, and by 1868 Lipscomb was the sole editor. Lipscomb (1831-1917) continued to edit the *Advocate* for more than 45 years, and through those years he exerted a greater influence on churches of Christ in the South than any other man. Lipscomb was thoroughly conservative in spirit. He had attended Franklin College, and the influence of Tolbert Fanning is obvious in Lipscomb's opposition to missionary societies and instrumental music and in his views on civil government.

Lipscomb, assisted by such co-editors as E. G. Sewell and F. D. Srygley, made his greatest contribution to the church in the South through the *Advocate,* but his activity was not limited to this. He was a respected preacher, though his simply expository sermons were quite different from the usual sermons of the time. Lipscomb had many ties with Texas churches, included a "Texas Department" in the *Advocate*, and wrote extensively about the missionary society when this issue brought Texas churches to the point of division in the 1880's. Lipscomb helped found Fanning Orphan School in 1884, after Fanning's death, and served on its Board for the rest of his life. He founded Nashville Bible School (now David Lipscomb College) in 1891 with a faculty consisting of himself, his brother William, and James A. Harding. Later Lipscomb write, "I have found more satisfaction in teaching the Bible to the young men and women at school than in any work of my life."

Lipscomb's editorials in the *Advocate* ranged over all the major questions that were raised in the church for nearly fifty years, and his conservative point of view often involved him in controversy. In 1866 Lipscomb and Isaac Errett discussed the Christian's relationship to government at length. Lipscomb wrote many articles in opposition to the missionary society. He believed that the church's work should be done through the local congregation and charged that the missionary society was a substitute for the divine plan. Discussing this point with J. W. McGarvey, Lipscomb wrote that if the society could do the church's missionary work, societies could do the church's other work – and the church would become "an empty, meaningless form, and sounding brass, emasculated of its spirit, divested of its sanctity, and its authority and usefulness are gone forever."

Lipscomb possessed one quality which is most impressive in his writings – an unwavering child-like faith in the Bible. If there was ever a man who bowed in resolute faith before the written Word, it must have been Lipscomb. On his fortieth anniversary as editor of the *Advocate,* he wrote, "The cardinal thought in my religion has ever been to follow the will of God, as expressed in precept or by approved example; to stand on safe ground; to be sure of the approval and blessing of God." Many years earlier (1867) Lipscomb had engaged in a written debate with Thomas Munnell on the missionary society. Lipscomb had said that 10,000 churches could scripturally cooperate, and Munnell asked him to describe how that many churches could cooperate in a businesslike way without some kind of organization. Lipscomb's reply reflects the spirit of his life, for he told Munnell, "We do not know that God proposed to convert the world in a businesslike way. Wise men, intent on the accomplishment of a great object, would scarcely choose a babe, born out of wedlock, cradled in a manger, as the efficient superintendent in the accomplishment of that work." Businessmen "would have hardly sought out unlearned, simple hearted fishermen as their agents, would not have chosen the infamy of the cross, and the degradation of the grave. This is so unbusinesslike that, businessmen entering in strive to change it to a more businesslike manner." And Lipscomb concluded, "God's ways are not man's ways, for the foolishness of God is wiser than man."

This was David Lipscomb's greatest legacy to churches of Christ scattered across the South – a resolute faith in the authority of God's Word.

J. W. McGarvey and Moses Lard

There are at least two other men who should be included among the influential brotherhood editors in the decade after the Civil War – J. W. McGarvey and Moses Lard. There are several reasons why their names are often linked together. McGarvey and Lard both lived in Kentucky after the war, and they worked together on two journals: *Lard's Quarterly* and the *Apostolic Times*. And both men shared a mediating viewpoint on the controversial questions of the day; that is, they favored the missionary society but opposed instrumental music.

J. W. McGarvey (1829-1911) lived in Lexington, Kentucky, from 1862 until his death. Earlier, he had attended Bethany College and had spent ten years preaching in Missouri. McGarvey is usually remembered as a teacher, writer and preacher, rather than as an editor. He taught in the College of the Bible in Lexington for more than forty years and inspired hundreds of your preachers to love the text of the English Bible. McGarvey wrote a number of important books including the *Commentary on Acts* (1863, revised ed. 1892), *Lands of the Bible* (1881), *Evidences of Christianity* (1886), and *Authorship of Deuteronomy* (1902). And he wrote extensively to warn the brotherhood of the threat that "biblical criticism" posed to their faith. (Cf. Chapter 11)

Moses Lard (1818-1880) was reared in the deepest poverty but was determined to obtain an education and preach the gospel. He graduated from Bethany College, though not until after he was 30 years old. After college Lard spent more than a decade preaching in Missouri. Lard was a great preacher, so great that when he was at his best, there was no other preacher in the brotherhood who was his equal. Even during his lifetime, the eloquence of his sermons became legendary. When the Civil War came, Lard's pacifism brought great hardship to him and his family in Missouri, and at J. W. McGarvey's suggestion, Lard moved to Georgetown, Kentucky, in 1863. He was warmly received in Kentucky, and this enable him to begin a project which he had planned earlier: the publication of a quarterly journal, which he named *Lard's Quarterly*. The *Quarterly* continued for five years (1863-1868) and included essays by

Lard, McGarvey and others. The *Quarterly* is one of the finest pieces of religious journalism in the history of the Restoration Movement. But there were not enough subscribers to sustain a quarterly, and after it was discontinued, five Kentucky preachers – McGarvey, Lard, Robert graham, Winthrop Hopson and L. B. Wilkes – began a new weekly, the *Apostolic Times,* which the five edited jointly. The *Times* was especially important in the 1870's because of its strong stand against the use of instrumental music.

A pivotal year

For the Restoration Movement 1866 was a pivotal year. It was a key year in the history of the three great journals that would guide the church through the years ahead. The *Gospel Advocate* resumed publication, the *Christian Standard* was launched, and the *American Christian Review* reversed its editorial policy and began opposing the missionary society – all in 1866. That same year, Alexander Campbell died, and with his unifying influence gone, controversies seemed to erupt everywhere. There was sectional bitterness between Northern and Southern Christians. Among Northern Christians 1866 marked the beginning of a decade of controversy and alienation. When the decade was over, a split in the church had become inevitable. The editors who would play key roles in this decade of decision have been introduced in this chapter. The controversies will be the subject of our next chapter.

Questions for review and discussion

1. Explain the statement, "The Restoration Movement has not had bishops; it has had editors."

Story of the Restoration

Was this true during the decades before the Civil War?
2. What was Benjamin Franklin's attitude toward the missionary society?
3. Why was the *Christian Standard* begun? How did it differ from the *American Christian Review?*
4. What were the main issues between the *Christian Standard* and *Gospel Advocate?*
5. Give a brief sketch of the life of David Lipscomb.
6. What was Lipscomb's great legacy to the church in the South?
7. List some of J. W. McGarvey's important contributions to the church.
8. How was 1866 a pivotal year in restoration history?
9. Identify the following:
(1) American Christian Review
(2) Christian Standard
(3) Isaac Errett
(4) "Progressive religion"
(5) Nashville Bible School
(6) Lipscomb-Munnell debate
(7) Moses E. Lard
(8) Lard's Quarterly
(9) Apostolic Times
(10) College of the Bible
(11) Commentary on Acts

Chapter 10
The Decade of Decision

The ten years following the Civil War (1866-1875) were a crucial decade in the history of the Restoration Movement, particularly in the North. The *American Christian Review* and *Christian Standard* were often in controversy with one another, and their clashes revealed that two distinct parties were appearing within the church in the North.

The Louisville Plan

The first clash between Benjamin Franklin and Isaac Errett involved the missionary society. As it became obvious, early in 1867, that Franklin's *Review* was now anti-society, Errett began a vigorous defense of the society. But as opposition to the society became more widespread, its friends attempted to win the support of the opposition by making important changes in the society's constitution. The life memberships and life directorships, purchased with a contribution to the society, were abolished in 1868.

The Louisville Plan, involving far more radical changes in the structure of the society, was adopted in 1869. A thorough overhaul of the society's organization seemed the only possible way to bring peace to the brotherhood, and a committee of twenty was appointed to propose a new plan for doing missionary work. The committee's proposals for reorganizing the missionary society were adopted when the society met in Louisville, Kentucky, in October, 1869; hence the name "Louisville Plan."

The Louisville Plan disbanded the old missionary society, and in its place new missionary boards were set up at district, state and national levels. A secretary was appointed in each district, and it was his responsibility to visit the churches in his district and solicit funds for the support of mission work at all levels – local, state and worldwide. The most important feature of the Louisville Plan was its proposal for financing the work of the various boards. The district boards would use half of the funds they collected in the district and send half to the state boards. The state boards, in turn, would send half of what they received to the national board. However, J. W. McGarvey proposed an amendment which allowed each church to specify some other distribution of funds if they desired. In the end, this provision so deprived the national board of funds that it was powerless to carry on any missionary work.

The *Christian Standard*, as might be expected, gave strong editorial support to the new plan, and it pleaded that the new plan be given a fair test "unembarrassed by controversy." The man whose attitude toward the new plan was most important to its success was Benjamin Franklin, and he hailed it with enthusiastic praise. Franklin wrote that the Louisville Plan was not a missionary society patterned after "sectarian models" but was a simply and wise arrangement of churches for doing missionary work. Franklin's approval of the Louisville Plan appears rather naive. Compared with the old missionary society, the Louisville Plan was much more like an ecclesiastical structure, and it seems surprising that Franklin did not see this immediately. Perhaps he was tired of controversy and willing to grasp at a straw for the sake of unity. Whatever his motive, Franklin gave the Louisville Plan his support for two years. But by 1871, he observed that the churches were allowing only meager sums to go to the national board – not enough to pay its operating expenses. He concluded that the churches were saying that they could spend their mission funds more efficiently than the national board.

The instrumental music controversy

The "era of good feeling" that might have followed the Louisville Plan was quickly shattered by other controversies among the Northern Christians – one involving the use of instrumental music in worship, another the new building of the Central church in Cincinnati.

Instrumental music was not used, or its use even discussed, in the early days of the Restoration Movement. The first discussion of the question came in 1851, when a reader asked J. B. Henshall, editor of the *Ecclesiastical Reformer,* whether instrumental music might not add solemnity to worship. Henshall's reply was against instrumental music, but later he carried some articles by others favoring the instrument. Seeing these articles, John Rogers wrote Alexander Campbell and asked his opinion about instrumental music. Campbell's answer was brief and blunt. He states that if churches had "no real devotion or spirituality in them," instrumental music might be "an essential prerequisite to devotion." But he added, "To all spiritually minded Christians, such aids would be as a cow bell in a concert." After Campbell's statement, the question was not even discussed again for another ten years.

As far as is known, the first congregation to introduce instrumental music into the worship was the Midway, Kentucky, church. Dr. L. L. Pinkerton (one of the earliest liberals in the brotherhood) was the preacher at Midway, and around 1860 they began using a small melodeon. Writing in 1860, Pinkerton stated that as far as he knew, he was the only preacher in Kentucky who had advocated using instrumental music in the churches and the Midway congregation was the only one that had introduced it. The reason for its use at Midway was the poor singing, which was so bad, according to Pinkerton, that it would "scare even the rats from worship." But there was opposition to the instrument at Midway. One of the elders, Adam Hibler, and a negro slave removed the offending melodeon through a window of the church building, but later it was returned.

The first extended discussion of the music question came in 1864-1865. W. K. Pendleton, editor of the *Millennial Harbinger* after Campbell, conceded that instrumental music was not used during the early centuries of the Christian era. But to Pendleton, it was a question of "mere expediency." The main participants in the 1864-1865 discussion were A. S. Hayden and J. W. McGarvey, and Hayden agreed with Pendleton that it was a question of expediency. Not McGarvey. He wrote, "In the earlier years of the present Reformation, there was entire unanimity in the rejection of instrumental music from our public worship. It was declared unscriptural, inharmonious with the Christian institution, and a source of corruption." And McGarvey never receded from those views. For more than two decades he wrote frequent articles arguing that it was unscriptural to use instrumental music. Eventually McGarvey realized that most churches in Kentucky and the North were determined to use the organ, and he turned his pen to biblical criticism and other subjects; but McGarvey always believed the instrument was wrong and refused to be a member of a congregation using it. He hoped that Broadway Christian Church in Lexington, where he had served as preacher and elder, would abstain from using the instrument during his lifetime. But in this he was "painfully disappointed," as he described it in his *Autobiography*. When Broadway began using the organ in 1903, McGarvey moved to another congregation. Ironically, when McGarvey died in 1911, an organ was used at his funeral service. An elderly Christian woman is said to have commented, "This is a great wrong, for he opposed it all his life."

Moses E. Lard was another unyielding opponent of the instrument. In 1864 he called the organ "a defiant and impious innovation on the simplicity and purity of the ancient worship." And Lard advised the brotherhood how to deal with the problem. First, every preacher should resolve never to enter a church containing an organ. Second, no Christian who had moved from a congregation should ever unite with one using an organ. And third, Lard advised that whenever a church introduced an organ, those who opposed it should abandon the church immediately. Through this course of action, Lard believed, "These organ grinding churches will in the lapse of time be broken down, or wholly apostatize, and the sooner they are in fragments the better for the cause of Christ."

In 1868 Benjamin Franklin estimated that there were about 10,000 churches in the brotherhood and that not more than fifty of these were using the instrument; but despite the opposition of Franklin, McGarvey, Lard and many others, other congregations began to introduce the instrument in the early 1870's. It was usually in the larger urban churches that the organ first appeared – an indication, perhaps, that social and economic influences played a part in the growing use of instrumental music. Occasionally the introduction of the organ resulted in a situation that would have been comic if it had not been such a disruptive influence on the church. In St. Louis, Missouri, for example, the church bought an Episcopalian church building in 1867 that had an organ in it, but the church was opposed to its use; whereupon a pro-organ party withdrew in disgust and built Central Christian Church, which had no organ. Thus the anti-organ congregation had an instrument but would not use it, while the pro-organ church had none.

The *Christian Standard* carried many articles on both sides of the music question in the late 1860's, but after Isaac Errett revealed his own views in a series of editorials in 1870, he found himself in another bitter controversy with Franklin. Errett's editorials counseled the churches against introducing instrumental music, but the basis of this counsel was the law of love. Errett realized that many Christians were conscientiously opposed to the instrument and that its use would disrupt the unity of the church. He paraphrased a proverb, "Better is poor singing where love is, than the grandest tones of the organ and hatred therewith." On the other hand, Errett argued that there was no law against organs, and stated, "We have no conscientious scruples against the use of instruments." Franklin realized that if brotherhood attitudes changed, Errett's advice that churches not use the organ might change. He wrote, "We put it on no ground of *opinion*, or *expediency*. The acts of worship are all prescribed in the law of God." Franklin was standing for the earlier principles of the Restoration Movement as he argued that the New Testament prescribed the church's worship and that instrumental music was an unauthorized innovation. Furthermore, Franklin saw the instrument as a symptom of deeper changes that were occurring in the church. He called the organ "the accompaniment of lifeless, formal and fashionable churches, in cities, where pride, aristocracy and selfishness prevail; where the poor have no sympathy, comfort or place."

It is interesting to note that while the organ was the focal point of bitter controversy in the North, David Lipscomb had little to say on the subject in the *Gospel Advocate*. The reason for this editorial silence was that the churches under Lipscomb's influence were already opposed to the organ and it was simply not an issue in the South; hence there was little need to discuss it. Lipscomb did chide men like McGarvey for what seemed an obvious inconsistency in opposing the organ so strongly but supporting the missionary society. Lipscomb thought that if he could open the door of expediency wide enough to admit the missionary society, he could take in the instrument with no extra effort.

Central Christian Church

The Central Christian Church in Cincinnati, Ohio, dedicated a new church building in February, 1872, and the new edifice immediately became the focal point for another bitter controversy among Northern Disciples. The new church was the largest in Cincinnati, seated over 2,000, and had the largest stained glass window in America. The building had cost over $140,000 and had an $8,000 organ, and to

Benjamin Franklin this was an unbearable extravagance. In a long editorial in the *Review* Franklin denounced the new building as a "temple of folly and pride" and declared that he would blush to speak of the "ancient order" or the "gospel restored" in such a place. The Central Church had used Baptist, Methodist and Congregationalist ministers in a week of preaching that opened the building, and Franklin saw this as proof that the church had made its peace with denominationalism. Franklin was particularly incensed at the introduction of the organ at Central. Charging that the church knew that "an overwhelming majority" of their brethren could not worship with the organ, Franklin wrote, "This is the kind of millstone they would hang about our necks to sink and disgrace us."

Inevitably, the missionary society and the Louisville Plan were engulfed in the controversy that swirled about the Central Church. The society had held many of its annual meetings in the church's old building, and the influential leaders of the missionary society were members of the Central Church. Franklin charged that when brethren came to Cincinnati to visit the center of their missionary work, they would be appalled that thousands of dollars had been "squandered in worldly show" and that the church's worship had been "corrupted". He concluded that when brethren saw what had happened to Cincinnati, they would not want that kind of gospel sent to anyone else.

The war of words over Central Church was more bitter and acrimonious than anything that had appeared previously in the *Standard* and *Review*. This indicated that the alienation between the conservative and progressive Disciples was becoming more serious with each new controversy.

Foreign Christian Missionary Society

In 1875 Isaac Errett and W. T. Moore took the lead in organizing the Foreign Christian Missionary Society. The Louisville Plan had been a dismal failure. While the substantial sums of money were being raised for mission work at the district level, very little was being sent on to the national board. There was not enough money to pay the overhead expenses, and no foreign missionary work was being done. Nor had the Louisville Plan ended the war of words. From 1872 onward Benjamin Franklin was attacking the Louisville Plan and citing its failure as evidence that the brotherhood did not want it.

Thus the Foreign Christian Missionary Society was born out of the failure of the Louisville Plan. Constitutionally, the new society was a return to the pattern of the 1849 society with paid memberships providing most of the funds for operating the society. Isaac Errett was elected president of the new society and continued in the office until his death in 1888. Financially, the foreign society was more successful than the Louisville Plan had ever been, and within a few years missions had been established in Denmark, England, France, Turkey, India, Japan and Panama.

The establishment of the new foreign society made it clear that the progressive Disciples in the North were determined to brush aside all opposition. R. M. Bishop, president of the old Louisville Plan society, stated in 1873 that there was no way to satisfy those who opposed the society. Bishop believed that men like Franklin were "no longer oracles" in the brotherhood, as they had once been, and he said, "We need no longer wait on their cooperation." Similarly, W. T. Moore declared bluntly in 1875 that since some would not cooperate in anything, "I think we ought to say to all such that we cannot wait on them any longer." What this meant was that with the creation of the new society, division among Christians in the North had become inevitable. Only one more ingredient was needed for the division to become real – time.

Questions for review and discussion

1. Describe the Louisville Plan. Why was it adopted? What was Benjamin Franklin's attitude toward it?
2. What was Alexander Campbell's attitude toward instrumental music?
3. What were the main arguments for and against instrumental music?
4. Describe J. W. McGarvey's role in the music controversy.
5. How was each of the following involved in the music controversy?
    (1) L. L. Pinkerton
    (2) Midway, KY
    (3) Moses E. Lard
    (4) A. S. Hayden
    (5) Benjamin Franklin
    (6) Isaac Errett
6. Discuss the controversy over the Central Christian Church building. How do you account for

the fact that a building could become the focal point of such bitterness?
7. What did the formation of the Foreign Christian Missionary Society mean in terms of brotherhood unity?

Chapter 11
The Lines of Division

The progessives win the North

Three decades after the establishment of the Foreign Christian Missionary Society, the United States Census bureau in 1906 listed the Christian Church and the Churches of Christ separately in its census reports. During those three decades the controversies between conservatives and progressives continued, churches divided, and the two sides drifted slowly apart. And during those decades the great majority of Christians in the North were won to the more liberal views of the progressives.

The progressives' victory was largely the work of two journals – the *Christian Standard* and the *Christian-Evangelist*. The *Christian-Evangelist* was began in 1882 through the merger of two earlier papers, and was edited jointly by J. H. Garrison and B. W. Johnson (author of the popular *People's New Testament with Notes*) until Johnson's death in 1894. Garrison then continued as sole editor until 1912. After the new paper was begun, it gave strong support to the missionary society and the growing use of instrumental music among the churches. The relations between the *Christian-Evangelist* and *Christian Standard* were cordial, and shortly before his death in 1888, Isaac Errett wrote that the two journals had been "the two most effectual instrumentalities" in winning acceptance for the missionary society. He added that he and J. H. Garrison had agreed on all points of "doctrine and practice and expediency."

Bill Humble, PhD.

Why did the great majority of the churches in the North accept the missionary society and instrumental music? The influence of Errett and Garrison was decisive, but this is not the whole story. While they were giving strong and vigorous leadership to the liberals, the conservatives lacked any comparable leadership after Benjamin Franklin's death in 1878 and fell to fighting among themselves. When Franklin died, John F. Rowe became editor of the *American Christian Review*. Eight years later, financial problems forced the *Review's* owner to offer it for sale, and editor Rowe hoped to buy the *Review* at less than its real worth. The owner refused to sell the paper on Rowe's terms, and Rowe resigned as editor and began a rival journal, the *Christian Leader,* a few months later. The *Review* was then purchased by Daniel Sommer, who had been disappointed at not being named Franklin's successor in 1878. Soon Sommer and Rowe were involved in a bitter personal feud, and the conservatives who had looked to the *Review* for leadership were badly divided.

Daniel Sommer (1850-1940) published the *Review* for over fifty years, but the paper was never what it had been under Benjamin Franklin's editorship. Sommer first changed its name to the *Octographic Review* and in 1914 to the *Apostolic Review*. But the changes went deeper. Sommer was ultra-conservative in spirit. Shortly before his death, he recalled an incident at Bethany College and said, "I denounced publicly the first deviation from apostolic simplicity that I found among 'disciples,' and I have been acting on the same principle ever since." And this was the story of Sommer's life – brotherhood critic. He believed that Christian colleges and orphan homes were unscriptural, and the opposed the "located preacher." These ideas came to be known as "Sommerism," and through the early decades of the twentieth century Sommerism seriously retarded the growth of the churches of Christ across the North.

The conservative South

The story in the South was quite different. The majority of the Southern churches had been committed to a more conservative understanding of the restoration plea as early as the 1850's. The most influential journal in the South was the *Gospel Advocate*." David Lipscomb edited the *Advocate* for nearly fifty years (1866-1912), and there was never a doubt about the conservative thrust of his teaching. There is no greater tribute to the influence of Lipscomb's work than the fact that when the final division came, most of the non-instrumental churches of Christ were located in the Southern states where the *Gospel Advocate* was widely read.

One of these states was Texas; and what happened in the Lone Star state was especially important, since churches of Christ were destined to become stronger in Texas than in any other state. There were many Tennesseans among the early settlers in Texas, both before and after the Civil war, and many of these were Christians who brought their *Gospel Advocates* with them. Except for Tennessee, the *Advocate* had its largest circulation in Texas, and for many years it contained a "Texas Department" edited by John T. Poe. And when Austin McGary established the *Firm Foundation* at Austin, Texas, in 1884, the *Advocate* had an ally in its opposition to the "innovations." McGary (1846-1928) was a native Texas who had had a colorful career as a frontier sheriff before he became a Christian.

The missionary society did not become a serious issue in Texas until the mid-1880's. Earlier, the churches had cooperated in supporting a "state evangelist," but the work had been under the oversight of one congregation, usually Sherman. C. M. Wilmeth was one of those who had served as "state evangelist." But in 1886 the progressives formed a Texas state missionary society, despite the opposition of men like Wilmeth, McGary, John T. Poe, R. M. Gano, Carroll Kendrick and others. The introduction of instrumental music followed in the wake of the missionary society in Texas. Prior to 1886, there were only a handful of Texas congregations using an organ, but many others introduced it within the next few years, often at the cost of a divided church. In 1896 J. D. Tant estimated that more than a hundred Texas congregations had divided over the use of instrumental music.

While the *Advocate* and *Firm Foundation* were united in opposing the society and organ, they took opposite sides on the question of rebaptism. The issue was whether one who had been immersed, but not specifically for the remission of sins, had to be rebaptized to be accepted as a member of the church. Austin McGary thought that rebaptism was necessary while David Lipscomb opposed it. The question was discussed by the two editors over a period of several years.

The 1906 census

The United States Census Bureau gave official recognition to the reality of a division between the Christian

Churches and Churches of Christ in its 1906 religious census, which was published in 1910. On June 17, 1907, S. N. D. North, the Director of the Census, wrote David Lipscomb and asked whether there was "a religious body called 'church of Christ,' not identified with the Disciples of Christ, or any other Baptist body." And if there was such a church, North wanted information about its organization and principles, and how the Census Bureau could secure a complete list of the churches. Replying to North's letter, Lipscomb outlined the basic principles of the Restoration Movement as formulated in Thomas Campbell's *Declaration and Address*. Next, Lipscomb charged that these principles had been betrayed when the society and instrument were introduced and that division had resulted. But Lipscomb explained:

The polity of the churches being purely congregational, the influences work slowly and the division comes gradually. The parties are distinguished as they call themselves "conservatives" and "progressives," as they call each other "antis" and "digressives."

In many places the differences have not as yet resulted in separation. There are some in the conservative churches in sympathy with the progressives, who worship and work with the conservatives because they have no other church facilities. The reverse of this is also true. Many of the conservatives are trying to appropriate the name "churches of Christ" to distinguish themselves from "Christian or Disciples' Churches."

A few months later, North visited the *Advocate* office and arranged for J. W. Shepherd, one of Lipscomb's co-editors, to compile a list of the churches of Christ for the census report. The Shepherd count was inexact, but even so, the 1906 census revealed two significant facts about the division in the Restoration Movement.

First, the Christian Churches were the larger body. The census report listed 8,293 churches and 982,701 members for the Christian Churches, while the churches of Christ had only 2,649 churches and 159, 658 members. Second, it was clear that the Christian Churches had won the North, while the churches of Christ found their numbers concentrated in the South. In the band of states stretching from Ohio to Kansas and Nebraska (the heartland of the Restoration Movement), the Disciples outnumbered the churches of Christ by 534,695 to 31,883, a ratio of 19 to 1. The same 19 to 1 ratio prevailed in the Atlantic seaboard states from Maine to Florida.

The ten states in which the churches of Christ had their largest membership are listed below (with the membership of the Christian Churches in the same states for comparative purposes):

1. Tennessee – Church of Christ membership: 41,411
Christian Church membership: 14,904
2. Texas – Church of Christ membership: 34,006
Christian Church membership: 39,550
3. Kentucky – Church of Christ membership: 12,451
Christian Church membership: 123,659
4. Arkansas – Church of Christ membership: 11,006
Christian Church membership: 10,269
5. Indiana – Church of Christ membership: 10,259
Christian Church membership: 108,188.
6. Alabama – Church of Christ membership: 9,214
Christian Church membership: 8,756

7. Oklahoma – Church of Christ membership: 8,074
Christian Church membership: 24,232
8. Missouri – Church of Christ membership: 7,087
Christian Church membership: 159,050
9. Ohio – Church of Christ membership: 4,954
Christian Church membership: 83,833
10. Illinois – Church of Christ membership: 3,552
Christian Church membership: 101,516

Ten years later in 1916, the churches of Christ were stronger than the Christian Churches in Texas, with 71,542 members compared with 54,836 for the Disciples. Also, Texas had surpassed Tennessee as the state where the churches of Christ had their largest membership.

Why the division?

Why did the Restoration Movement suffer division?

(1) the long controversy focused on the missionary society and instrumental music, but the basic problem underlying these two issues was the rise of two antagonistic interpretations of the restoration principle. Alexander Campbell had formulated the strict view in the *Christian Baptist,* when he insisted that the New Testament was a blueprint for the church and that any practice not specified in this pattern was forbidden. Later, as the movement grew and the first traces of a denominational mentality began to appear, many interpreted the restoration principle less rigidly by allowing many practices as "expedients." The basic issue was the same whether the practice in question was the society or the organ. They were defended by some as "expedients," and opposed by others as unauthorized by the New Testament pattern. Moses Lard proved to be correct

when he warned in 1869 that expediency might be the rock on which the Restoration Movement went to pieces. at lease, it was one of the rocks.

(2) Sectionalism and Civil War bitterness were another factor. The churches in the South, it will be remembered, had turned against the Cincinnati missionary society during the 1850's, but this had not produced any real feeling of alienation between them and Northern Christians. But when sectional feelings were added to the doctrinal disagreements, the sense of oneness was shattered.

(3) Another factor, particularly in the North, was the growing social and economic differences among the Christians, frontier and rural conservatism set against urban demands for a more dignified and progressive religion. The sociologist of religion would describe it as the evolution of a denominational spirit. The new denominational spirit, symbolized by leaders like Errett and Garrison, favored a looser interpretation of the restoration principle and came to think of the movement as a denomination among denominations. The other spirit, symbolized by Franklin and Lipscomb, was committed to the past and to a narrower view of the restoration plea; and it was firm in its conviction that their brotherhood was not another denomination but was, in truth, the one true church restored.

Liberalism in the Christian Church

While it was still in the process of dividing from the churches of Christ, the Christian Church began to feel the strain of serious internal tensions. The key to the problem was theological liberalism. The new liberal theology and biblical criticism, which had arisen in Germany through the

Story of the Restoration

work of such scholars as Schleirmacher, Wellhausen, Ritschl and Harnack, was widely accepted by American Protestants in the 1880's and 1890's. And the Christian Church was unable to escape the challenge of the new thought. Alexander Proctor and George W. Longan, prominent Missouri preachers, were among the first to accept some of the conclusions of biblical criticism. In 1889 Dr. R. C. Cave of St. Louis shocked the brotherhood with a sermon which openly denied such fundamental doctrines as the virgin birth and bodily resurrection of the Lord. But the brotherhood was not ready for such ideas, and Cave soon left the church. However, after the Disciples Divinity House was established at the University of Chicago in 1894, many young Christians began doing graduate work at Chicago and at Yale, and as a result, theological liberalism was soon widespread among the Disciples. The liberals had a strong editorial champion after 1908 when Charles Clayton Morrison became editor of the *Christian Century*. Later, the *Christian Century* severed its ties with the Disciples and became the voice of liberal Protestantism in America.

Meanwhile, the *Christian Standard* took a determined stand against the new liberalism. J. W. McGarvey began a regular column on "Biblical Criticism" in the *Standard* in 1893 and continued it until his death. McGarvey was 64 years old when he began this work, but even so, he read extensively in critical literature and mastered the liberals' views. His approach to biblical criticism was typical of his whole bent of mind – he studied the conclusions of biblical criticism with great thoroughness, concluded that they jeopardized New Testament teaching about salvation, and were incompatible with biblical faith. He never retreated from that conclusion. The *Christian-Evangelist* and *Christian Century* both came in for sharp criticism, but McGarvey did not stop there. The most prominent scholars in America – Charles A. Briggs, William Rainey Harper, Lyman Abbott, Washington Gladden and George Foote Moore – were scornfully attacked. But McGarvey's message was not really addressed to the scholar. It was for the average Christian to warn him that biblical critics were a threat to his faith.

The *Christian Standard* and *Christian-Evangelist* had stood together when the issues were the missionary society and instrumental music. But as the new liberalism appeared, the two journals moved apart. The *Christian-Evangelist* was more open to biblical criticism than the *Standard*. When the Federal Council of Churches was launched in 1908, the Disciples of Christ became members. J. H. Garrison supported this decision, while the *Standard* opposed it. Next, the activities of the missionary society became a serious issue in the 1920's. When it became known that the society's missionaries were practicing "open membership" in the mission fields (accepting members without immersion), the *Standard* turned against the society, and decades of stormy controversy followed. As a result the Christian Church has now been divided into two rival fellowships. The liberal group is the International Convention of Christian Churches (Disciples of Christ) whose headquarters are in Indianapolis. The *Christian-Evangelist,* now named *The Christian*, is their official journal. The more conservative group so usually called the "independent" or "conservative" Christian Churches. The

Christian Standard is their most influential journal. Each group has approximately one million members.

Questions for review and discussion

1. How do you account for the fact that Christian Churches were so much stronger than the churches of Christ in the North?
2. Where were the churches of Christ strong numerically? How do you account for this?
3. Discuss David Lipscomb's role in having Christian Churches and churches of Christ listed separately in the 1906 census.
4. Why did the Restoration Movement suffer division?
5. Describe the rise of liberalism in the Christian Church. What effect has this had on the Christian Church?
6. Identify the following:
   (1) J. H. Garrison
   (2) Daniel Sommer
   (3) Christian Evangelist
   (4) Christian Century
   (5) The Christian
   (6) John F. Rowe
   (7) Austin McGary
   (8) Disciples Divinity House
   (9) "Biblical Criticism"
   (10) "Conservative" Christian Churches
   (11) "Open membership"

Bill Humble, PhD.

Chapter 12: Twentieth Century Growth

The churches of Christ have experienced a remarkable growth in the twentieth century. They have increased from 159,658 members in 190 to 317,937 in 1916. This was a growth of more than 100% in a single decade, though some allowance must be made for the incompleteness of the 1906 count. By 1926 the churches of Christ had grown to 433,714, a 50% growth over the previous census. But the strength of the churches was still concentrated in the South with Texas, Tennessee, Arkansas and Oklahoma leading the list in that order.

It is difficult to obtain accurate statistics for the growth of the church after 1926. The 1936 religious census was so incomplete that nearly all churches showed sharp declines in total membership (the churches of Christ from 433,714 in 1926 to 309,551 in 1936). The statistics were so unsatisfactory that the government discontinued its religious census after 1936.

The best estimates are that the total membership had grown to 2,250,000 or 2,500,000 by the late 1960's. The *Yearbook of American Churches for 1967* lists the membership of churches of Christ at 2,350,000. In 1967 Louis Cassels, Religion Editor for United Press International, called the churches of Christ the "fastest growing major religious body in the United States."

But numbers do not tell the full story of the dynamic growth of the churches of Christ. The larger and more expensive buildings, the more affluent middle-class membership, the number of full time ministers, the increasing emphasis on Bible schools and Christian education, and missionary outreach all reflect a gradual but impressive growth. As the century began, the churches of Christ were large rural and had small frame buildings and preaching once-a-month. The larger urban congregations had nearly all gone with the Christian Church. The rural character of the churches of Christ is obvious in the 1926 religious census. Of 6,226 congregations (with an average membership of 70) listed in the census report, 5,330 were classified as "rural." But by the 1940's many more congregations were appearing in the larger towns and cities. After World War II the church enjoyed a remarkable growth in urban areas. As its members climbed the economic and educational ladder, the church moved "across the tracks." The small frame building with a few Bible classes meeting in different corners of the auditorium disappeared. Thousands of new church buildings were erected, some costing hundreds of thousands of dollars with adequate educational facilities.

There were many great preachers who contributed to the twentieth century grown of the church. Early in the century there were such men as M. C. Kurfees, Price Billingsley, George Klingman, C. R. Nichol, A. G. Freed, James A. Harding and G. Dallas Smith. Kurfees spent many years preaching for the Campbell Street church in Louisville, Kentucky, and is remembered for his book *Instrumental Music in Worship*. Klingman delivered a series of lectures in Abilene, Texas, in 1907, forerunners of the Abilene Christian College lectureship. C. R. Nichol engaged in many religious debates, as did J. D. Tant, J. W. Chism, Joe Warlick and others.

By the 1930's and 1940's N. B. Hardeman, G. C. Brewer and Foy E. Wallace, Jr. were among the most influential preachers in the church. Hardeman is remembered for the great "Hardeman tabernacle meetings" in Nashville, Tennessee. The first was held in 1922 in Ryman Auditorium and attracted unprecedented crowds. The religious debate was still very popular in the 1930's and 1940's, and the Hardeman-Bogard, Brewer-Lindsey and Wallace-Norris debates were among those that excited widespread brotherhood interest. And while debating is not as popular as it once was, the 1967 debate between William S. Banowsky and Anson Mount on the "Playboy philosophy" is proof that a timely controversy still arouses public interest.

The Bible school has played a very important role in the twentieth century growth of the churches of Christ. Jesse P. Sewell was one of the first to see the possibilities of congregational development through adequate classes. Sewell went to the Grove Avenue church in San Antonio, Texas in 1927 and planned an education program far in advance of anything the brotherhood had seen before.

Journals

The influence of the religious journals – always a key factor in restoration history – has continued through the twentieth century. It will be remembered that the *Gospel Advocate* and *Firm Foundation* supplied leadership to the churches that opposed the society and instrument in the late 1800's, and these two journals have continued to be the most influential among churches of Christ through the twentieth century. The *Gospel Advocate* has had many great men on its editorial staff including M. C. Kurfees, E.

A. Elam, H. Leo Bowles, Foy E. Wallace, Jr. and B. C. Goodpasture. The *Firm Foundation* was edited by G. H. P. Showalter from 1908 until his death in 1954. Reuel Lemmons became editor of the *Firm Foundation* in 1955, and under his leadership the *Foundation* has been a stabilizing "middle-of-the-road" influence in the church.

Many other journals have contributed to the growth of the churches of Christ. The *Christian Leader*, another journal which began in the 1800's, exerted a strong influence in the North. It was edited by F. L. Rowe for many years. The *Christian Worker* began publication in Wichita, Kansas, in 1915 and was widely read through the Midwest. It was edited by Rue Porter through the 1940's and 1950's. The *Christian Chronicle* was founded in 1942 by Olan Hicks, who continued as its editor for 12 years. The *Chronicle* was an important milestone in brotherhood journalism. Earlier journals had carried "news and notes," but their main contents were doctrinal and inspirational writings, whereas the *Chronicle* was intended to report the news of the brotherhood. The *Twentieth Century Christian,* edited by Norvel Young, has featured shorter inspirational articles and has enjoyed a wide circulation. Other journals – such as *Christian Woman, Teenage Christian, Christian Bible Teacher* and *Power for Today* – have been designed to fill special needs in the church.

Christian Colleges

The Christian colleges have also been an important factor in the twentieth century expansion of the churches of Christ; but the leaders of the church were so committed to Christian education that they made one tragic mistake. During the years between 1900 and 1930 they established far too many schools, and most of them faced an impossible struggle for survival. Lockney Christian College, Gunter Bible School, Clebarro College and Sabinal Christian College were among the early Texas colleges which failed. The crash of 1929 brought acute financial problems to all Christian colleges, and the decade of the 1930's witnessed the closing of Thorp Spring Christian College, Cordell Christian College and Burritt College. Burritt College, located at Spencer, Tennessee, had been in operation since 1849, while Thorp Spring had been serving Texas Christians for more than half a century.

By 1940 the brotherhood had five colleges which had survived the depression years. (1) David Lipscomb College, founded in 1891 by David Lipscomb as Nashville Bible School, was the oldest. (2) Freed-Hardeman College, Henderson, Tennessee, was founded by A. G. Freed and N. B. Hardeman in 1908. (3) Abilene Christian College (called Childers Classical Institute until 1920) was founded by A. B. Barret in 1906. The annual Bible lectureship began in 1918 and has become the largest annual gathering of members of the churches of Christ. The college moved to its present location "on the hill" in 1929. Guided by President Don Morris and Dean Walter Adams for more than a quarter century, Abilene hs become the largest of the Christian colleges with an enrollment of more than 3,000. (4) Harding College began in 1924 through the merger of Harper College, Harper, Kansas (1915-1924) and Arkansas Christian College at Morrilton, Arkansas. Harding moved to its present location in Searcy in 1934. (5) Pepperdine College in Los Angeles was begun in 1937 and is named for its chief benefactor, George Pepperdine, a Christian businessman who founded the Western Auto Co. In 1940 these five schools had a total enrollment of less than 2,000. Only Pepperdine was accredited, and none offered graduate work.

The growth of Christian colleges since World War II has more than matched the growth of churches of Christ. All the older colletes have achieved full accreditation, and Abilene, Harding and Pepperdine now have graduate schools. More than a score of new schools have sprung up in many parts of the United States. These include Oklahoma Christian, Lubbock Christian, York, Alabama Christian, Christian College of the Southwest, Fort Worth Christian and Michigan Christian. The Christian colleges now enroll nearly 15,000 students annually.

Controversial Issues

The twentieth century has brought its problems as well as growth. Several controversial issues have strained the church's oneness.

Anti-Sunday School. Whether it was scriptural for a church to have Sunday School classes was discussed just after 1900. The issue was more serious in Texas than elsewhere. Two of the early Texas colleges, Lockney and Gunter, were operated by those who opposed Bible classes, and this was one reason for their failure. Ultimately, a very great majority of the churches accepted the Bible classes as an expedient, and invaluable, means of teaching. But a tiny minority of churches has continued to regard classes as unscriptural.

Bill Humble, PhD.

Premillennialism. Premillennialism is the doctrine that Christ will reign for 1,000 years over an earthly kingdom following his second coming. The question was first raised in 1914-1915 when R. H. Boll began teaching premillennialism in his front page editorials in the *Gospel Advocate.* Boll was dropped from the *Advocate* staff, but in 1916 he became editor of *Word and Work,* and this journal has continued to represent the millennial view. Boll's views precipitated a stormy controversy which plagued the church for twenty years. Two milestones in the controversy were a written debate between Boll and H. Leo Boles (1928) and an oral debate between Foy E. Wallace, Jr. and Charles M. Neal (1933). Wallace led the struggle against premillennialism in the church, and more than any other preacher, was responsible for its ultimate rejection. Louisville, Kentucky was the center of brotherhood premillennialism, though for several years Harding College was under a cloud of suspicion for suspected premillennial sympathies.

Sommerism. The views of Daniel Sommer – opposition to located preachers, colleges and orphan homes – have troubled the church in the North throughout the twentieth century. W. Carl Ketcherside and Leroy Garrett were the champions of these views in the 1940's and 1950's and refused fellowship to those who would not accept their ultraconservative views. But Ketcherside and Garrett have done an about-face in the 1960's and now plead for a wider fellowship that will include all who stand in the restoration tradition without regard to doctrinal differences.

War Questions. The question whether a Christian can take life in the military service of his country has been a frequent topic of debate among churches of Christ; but the issue has not been made a test of fellowship, and the final answer has been left to the individual's conscience. David Lipscomb's pacifism continued to have a strong influence over brotherhood thought through the Word War I era, and most journal articles insisted that Christians could not bear arms. In 1926, 450 preachers responded to a survey question, "Do you believe that a Christian can scripturally take human life in war?" and there were only 24 "yes" responses. But during World War II a sharper division of brotherhood thought appeared, and one influential journal, the *Bible Banner,* championed the view that a Christian could accept military service. It should be added, however, that during both world wars most Christian men disregarded the pacifism in the pulpit and served in the armed forces. The conscientious objector was the rare exception, not the rule.

Congregational Cooperation. The most serious issue that churches of Christ have faced this century is church cooperation and "insitutionalism." Led by Roy Cogdill, Yater Tant and the *Gospel Guardian,* a substantial number of churches have come to oppose such cooperative programs of evangelism as the *Herald of Truth* and the homes for orphans and aged, as they are presently organized. During the past 15 years many debates have been held, churches have divided, and fellowship has been broken. This is the most serious division, numbers wise, that churches of Christ have suffered. Whether the division is final, or whether it can be healed, is yet to be determined.

World Missions

The awakening of the churches of Christ to the call of world missions in the mid-twentieth century has been one of the most remarkable signs of their spiritual vitality. Earlier in the century there were only feeble efforts at missionary work. J. M. McCaleb went to Japan in 1892. Three decades later he reported that a total of 33 Americans had worked in Japan and that 1,000 had been baptized. The church in Japan with less than 1,000 members was the seventh largest Protestant body in Japan. Other countries where early mission work was attempted were India, Persia, South Africa and Mexico. John Sherriff, converted in Australia, went to South Africa as a missionary before the turn of the century. The W. N. Shorts established a mission at Sinde, Rhodesia, in 1923.

The cause of missions was weakened through the 1920's because of its ties with premillennialism. The Highland church in Louisville, Kentucky, was a leader in encouraging missionary work; yet it was known to be a premillennial congregation, and R. H. Boll and Don Carlos Janes were both associated with Highland. It seemed that when missionaries returned to the United States for visits, they inevitable went to Highland. Thus the brotherhood came to suspect that the missions in Japan, India and perhaps Africa were premillennial, and this fear reinforced their apathy toward the support of missions. When J. W. Shepherd published a missions' directory in 1931, he could list only 29 missionaries. They were working in Africa, China, Japan, Korea, the Philippines and Brazil.

The great missionary expansion of churches of Christ has come since World War II. The most important reason for this awakening has been the scattering of thousands of Christians, most of them servicemen, to the ends of the earth – a modern *diaspora*. These servicemen have established congregations, have become missionaries after their tour of military duty was finished, and have awakened countless churches in the United States to a sense of duty. The "enemy countries" of World War II became the targets of the first missionary work. Otis Gatewood and the Broadway church in Lubbock aroused others, and the church was planted in Germany (1947), Japan (1947) and Italy (1949). These beginnings encouraged others to follow and churches were planted in every major country of Europe except Portugal.

The post-war missionary awakening has been crowned with some amazing successes. In Nigeria, an American correspondence course sparked an indigenous restoration movement that resulted in thousands of conversions. The first American missionaries arrived in 1952 and a decade later the church in Nigeria had over 40,000 members. The first attempt at group evangelism came in 1961 with an "exodus" of 13 families to Sao Paulo, Brazil. (It is interesting to note, however, that an "exodus" had been attempted more than 60 years earlier, when C. M. Wilmeth led a group to Tampico, Mexico in 1897.) India has been another field "white unto the harvest," and Canadian missionaries working in India since 1963 have baptized thousands in the Assam and Madras areas.

Today the churches of Christ have about 350 missionary families in more than 80 nations.

Questions for review and discussion

1. What was the approximate membership of the church of Christ in 1906? In 1916? In 1926? Today? What has been responsible for this growth?

Bill Humble, PhD.

2. Explain the statement, "The Restoration Movement has not had bishops; it has had editors." Has this been true in the twentieth century?
3. List six of our present journals. How is each contributing to the growth of the church?
4. Name the five Christian colleges in existence in 1940. Why have so many new schools begun since 1940? Name as many of the new schools as you can.
5. How has the church benefited from the work of the Christian colleges?
6. What problems do our Christian colleges face?
7. List some of the main controversies in the church. Which have been problems in the part of the United States where you live?
8. Why has there been such a sharp increase in mission work since World War II? (List as many reasons as you can.)
9. What mission work has our congregation supported?
10. Identify each of the following:
    (1) George Klingman
    (2) Hardeman tabernacle meetings
    (3) Foy E. Wallace, Jr.
    (4) Jesse P. Sewell
    (5) Burritt College
    (6) George Pepperdine
    (7) Premillennialism
    (8) R. H. Boll
    (9) Sommerism
    (10) Gospel Guardian

Story of the Restoration

(11) a modern *diaspora*
(12) "Exodus"
(13) Nigeria
(14) Otis Gatewood

Chapter 13:
The Continuing Restoration

What is the status of the Restoration Movement today? What is the restoration principle? Is the goal of a restored New Testament church still accepted as valid?

There are now three major religious bodies whose historic roots are in the Stone-Campbell restoration of the early 1800's: (1) Disciples of Christ, (2) "Independent" or "Conservative" Christian Churches, and (3) churches of Christ. These groups now hold opposite views as to the validity of the restoration principle.

Disciples of Christ

The leadership of the Disciples of Christ (the liberal wing of the Christian Church) has now abandoned the concept of restoring New Testament Christianity. They believe that in the light of modern scholarship it is no longer possible to accept the New Testament as a pattern for the church, and thus the whole nineteenth century effort to restore the church was an impossible search for an illusion. If this is correct, it follows that the work of Campbell, Stone and McGarvey must be dismissed as well intended but wrong. And this is exactly how the Disciples' leaders feel about the past.

Dr. Ronald Osborn, Dean of Christian Theological Seminary and past president of the Disciples' International Convention, is quite frank in his repudiation of the restoration concept. As one of the editors of a three volume restudy of the Disciples (1963), Dr. Osborn wrote, "Many of the papers constituting this volume and the two succeeding volumes in this series explicitly repudiate restorationism, as do numerous other studies recently written by Disciple scholars. As an interpretation of apostolicity, restoration is no longer tenable" (*The Reformation of Tradition,* p. 318). Dr. Ralph Wilburn, Dean of Lexington Theological Seminary, wrote in the same volume, "The restoration idea is basically a false concept ... It would seem wise to abandon the use of the term altogether."

But if the restoration principle is repudiated, what happens to the distinctive practices once thought essential in a restored church? What about immersion? Weekly communion? Congregational independence? Writing in *Christian Century* (Sept. 25, 1963), Osborn said, "The biblical and theological scholarship of recent decades has made restoration untenable." And as a result, according to Osborn, "Most Disciples who have repudiated restorationism have no adequate basis for justifying their congregationalism, weekly communion, immersion-baptism, boards of elders and deacons (vestiges of a one-time lay ministry) or other distinctive practices." The Disciples of Christ are one of the denominations in the Consultation on Christian Unity whose aim is the merger of eight Protestant churches. The Disciples are now in a "restructure" movement that will end the old congregational freedom and create a denominational structure that can join such a merger. And what of such practices as immersion and the weekly observance of the Lord's Supper? These will be abandoned and the Disciples will disappear in an ecumenical church.

What has caused the Disciples to make such a radical break with the past? *The answer is theological liberalism!* The rise of liberalism among the Disciples has been discussed in an earlier chapter. (Review the last section of Chapter 11.) When the Disciples began sending men to Yale and Chicago for graduate work around the turn of the century, the prevailing climate of thought was extremely liberal. Amid such a climate the Disciples' historic plea for restoration seemed an untenable relic from the past. And so, within a single generation the Disciples' leadership was so molded in the image of liberalism that there remained no rationale for restoring New Testament Christianity. It should be axiomatic that the restoration principle demands a conservative view of the inspiration and authority of the Scripture. When the liberal sees his Bible as a fallible book (as Disciples do), how can he be concerned about restoring the church as it was in the New Testament? Why restore what might be fallible? Thus, when the Disciples became theologically liberal, their quest for New Testament Christianity became as illusory as the pot of gold at the end of the rainbow.

"Independent" Christian Churches

The "Independent" or "Conservative" Christian Churches do not share the Disciples' liberalism. Rather, they are so opposed to the Disciples' break with the past and "restructure" movement that the division between them and the Disciples is becoming final. The "Independents" publish an annual *Directory of the Ministry,* listing their churches and preachers. A recent edition listed 4,456 congregations with an estimated membership of 1,008,988.

Story of the Restoration

The "Independents" are strongest in Indiana, Ohio, Illinois, Kentucky and Missouri. They have an annual "North American Christian Convention," similar to our Christian college lectureships, which attracts more than 15,000 each year. The "Independents" have near 400 missionaries, all supported directly by churches, and more than 30 Bible colleges for training preachers. Doctrinally, the "Independents" are very conservative and just as committed to the restoration principle as churches of Christ. They practice baptism for the remission of sins, weekly communion, free churches overseen by elders, and often wear the name "church of Christ." The most important difference between "Independents" and the churches of Christ is their use of instrumental music.

How should members of the churches of Christ regard these "Independents"? As brethren in Christ – brethren whose worship they cannot conscientiously fellowship, it is true, but still their brethren in Christ.

Churches of Christ

The churches of Christ are still committed to the restoration ideal – but there are serious questions about their future. Can they remain conservative theologically? Will they continue to believe in the restoration principle? And if they do, how will they view the work of restoration? A task completed by past generations? Or a continuing challenge which confronts each generation anew?

When the history of the churches of Christ since 1906 is compared with that of the Disciples, there are significant differences. One difference is the remarkable growth of the churches of Christ. (Cf. Chapter 12) Only one sixth as large as the Christian Church in 1906, the churches of Christ are now larger (with 2,350,000 members) than the Disciples and "Independents" combined (1,918,471 members). (*Yearbook of American Churches*)This growth cannot be explained apart from their biblical faith and commitment to the restoration ideal. The Disciples, on the other hand, illustrate the fact that liberal theology and dynamic numerical growth seem, somehow, to move in opposite directions.

Another difference has been the cultural isolation of the churches of Christ. They entered the twentieth century largely Southern, largely rural, and on the wrong side of the tracks. Early in the century the preacher with a college education would have been the exception, not the rule, among churches of Christ. Even after a substantial number of preachers began to receive an education in the Christian colleges, the number who had any graduate work was very small. The average preacher of the 1930's and 1940's knew his Bible and had a strong faith in the restoration principle. But he would have known little about Karl Barth and Emil Brunner, the rediscovery of Soren Kierkegaard, or the new dialectical theology. These were of no concern to him. Perhaps without realizing it, he had been living in cultural isolation.

Today the churches of Christ are emerging from their cultural isolation. The higher social, economic and educational levels in the average congregation indicate that they are becoming "middle class" and that continued isolation is neither possible nor desirable. The education of preachers shows that cultural isolation is passing. There is greater interest in graduate studies. The preacher or teacher with a doctorate was almost unknown among churches of Christ a

Story of the Restoration

generation ago, but today he is appearing in increasing numbers. This means that we now stand at a crossroad which is analogous, at least in some respects, with that at which the Disciples stood sixty years ago. Emerging from their cultural isolation, the Disciples were won to liberalism and repudiated the quest for the New Testament church.

What does the future hold for churches of Christ? Will they slowly fall under the influence of modernism? Question whether there is really a New Testament pattern for the church? As an increasing number of our members seek graduate education beyond our Christian colleges, some will become too liberal to remain within our fellowship. A substantial number have already done this. And the time may come when those who have abandoned the faith commonly held among churches of Christ will choose to remain in the pulpits of our churches, and when this time comes, the dangers will be intensified. The next ten or twenty years will be a testing time for churches of Christ, but if we are aware of the dangers that accompany the end of our cultural isolation, we have a better chance to surmount these dangers.

But if there are analogies between our position today and that of the Disciples around 1900, there are also differences: (1) We can profit from a half century of Disciples' history and be warned not to say, "It could never happen to us." (2) The theological climate is more conservative now than it was a half century ago. When the Disciples left their cultural isolation, liberalism was unchallenged. But in the fifty years that have elapsed since then, liberalism has been chastened by neo-orthodoxy, existentialism, a new interest in biblical theology, and the discoveries of biblical archaeologists. The whole mood of biblical and theological studies is somewhat more conservative now than it was a half century ago. (3) Our Christian colleges are doing a better job of introducing students to contemporary thought and preparing them for the issues they will confront in graduate studies. (4) The conservative cause has scholarly and articulate voices today, as in *Christianity Today,* which were lacking fifty years ago. And the cause for which these voices plead – the inspiration and authority of the Scripture – is the foundation upon which the restoration principle rests.

The future is a mixed mosaic. The crossroad at which we stand challenges us to serious soul searching and concern for the future. The brotherhood ostrich renders a disservice when he ignores the obvious. There are no real dangers in the end of our cultural isolation. The question yet to be answered is whether the faith that has brought us where we are will survive. But there are also unprecedented challenges and opportunities. If we can break out of our cultural isolation without the loss of our faith, and if we can raise up men of unwavering faith whose training will qualify them to approach classes we have never approached before, the Restoration Movement might yet make such an impact as the Campbells envisioned.

A Continuing Challenge

We must ask one more question. How successful has the work of restoration been? Has the church of the New Testament era really been restored? Fully restored? Or is its restoration a continuing challenge which calls each generation anew?

Story of the Restoration

The goal of a restored church implies that the church in every age must stand under the judgment of Holy Writ, ever striving to become what God would have it be, but ever falling short of this goal. Viewed from this perspective, restoration is a continuing challenge. Yet our heritage from the past should not be treated with contempt. We owe a great debt of gratitude to our spiritual forefathers; and if it is self-righteousness to assume that the work of restoration is complete and perfect, it is ingratitude to look with disdain on what we have received from the past. The truth is that the quest for a restored New Testament church has been a mixture of successes and shortcomings.

Let us note some examples of the successes:

(1) The immersion of believers was the exclusive practice of the early church. (Cf. Acts 8.36-39; Rom. 6.3,4; Col. 2.12). The believer's burial reenacted the burial and resurrection of his Savior. There was no sprinkling of infants in the New Testament church, nor will there be whenever it is restored. Furthermore, the immersion which was practiced in the first century was "for the remission of sins" and always stood between the sinner and salvation in New Testament teaching (Mark 16.16; Acts 2.38; 22.16; 1 Peter 3.21).

(2) The early Christians observed the Lord's supper on the first day of the week as a proclamation of their faith in the Lord's death "till he come" (Acts 20.7; 1 Cor. 11.23-29). Nor does the New Testament record their observing the supper at any other time.

(3) Vocal music – "singing and making melody with your heart" – was the early Christians' way of praising God (Eph. 5.19; Col. 3.16; 1 Cor. 14.15). There is no trace of

the use of instrumental music in Christian worship in either the New Testament or the apostolic fathers.

(4) The local churches in New Testament times were free and autonomous. Christ was honored as the head of the church, his word its only rule of faith and practice. There were two classes of officers in each church: bishops or elders exercised the oversight, and deacons were special servants.

There can be no New Testament church without such marks as believers' baptism and the oversight of elders; and the renewal of many such New Testament practices has carried us a long way toward the goal of the primitive church. Yet, as important as these marks of the true church are, they are outward observances and are not the sum total of discipleship. And it is possible that the Lord might say, "As you have tried to restore the church, you have stressed the outward observances like baptism, but you have left undone the weightier matters of the law like commitment and sacrifice and the life of prayer. These you ought to have done, but not left the others undone."

Let us note some of our failures – attitudes of the New Testament church which we have yet to restore:

(1) The early Christians were so committed to the Lord that they "continued steadfastly" in his service and joyfully accepted the loss of homes, or even life itself, for his sake. To live was Christ. This was the only thing in life that really mattered to them. When this commitment is contrasted with the widespread apathy in so many congregations today, can we be so sure that we have succeeded in restoring real New Testament Christianity?

Story of the Restoration

(2) The early Christians' concern for the Lord transcended their concern for material things. They could sell houses and lands and property and lay the money at the apostles' feet. The Corinthians' "deep poverty" did not prevent their sharing with others. When today's materialism stands in such sharp contrast with the attitude of the first Christians, can we really say, "We are just like the early church?"

(3) The early church was fervently evangelistic. Driven from their homes by persecution, they went everywhere preaching the word. Within a single generation the good news had been proclaimed in every corner of the Roman world. The early church accomplished so much with so little, and we have accomplished so little with so much. Have we really restored the missionary fervor of the early Christians?

(4) The Christians of the first century believed that there was power in prayer and that God truly answered their prayers. And they prayed. When the prayer life of the early church is compared with ours, can we really be so sure that we have restored the New Testament church?

The restoration of the New Testament church is a heritage which we have received from the past. But it is also a challenge which we face in the present. As long as the twentieth century church lacks the fervor and spirituality of the early Christians, as long as it is complacent and materialistic and apathetic to a lost world, the restoration of the New Testament church must be a continuing challenge which calls every single Christian anew.

Bill Humble, PhD.

Questions for review and discussion

1. Identify the Disciples of Christ. What is their attitude toward the restoration principle?
2. Why have the Disciples rejected the restoration concept?
3. How is our situation today similar to that of the Disciples around 1900? How is it different?
4. Do you think the churches of Christ will still accept the restoration principle twenty years from now?
5. Are the "Independent" Christian Churches more like the Disciples or the churches of Christ?
6. Do you think it possible that the "Independent" Christian Churches and churches of Christ might sometime unite?
7. Do you feel that we have really restored the New Testament church? Its worship? Its organization? Its terms of membership? Its commitment? Its spirituality? (You might spend a few minutes discussing each of these.)
8. Identify each of the following:
    (1) Dr. Ronald Osborn
    (2) "Restructure"
    (3) Consultation on Christian Unity
    (4) North American Christian Convention
    (5) "Cultural isolation"

www.ingramcontent.com/pod-product-compliance
Lightning Source LLC
Chambersburg PA
CBHW060801050426
42449CB00008B/1477